THE PATH OF THE RIGHTEOUS GENTILE

AN INTRODUCTION TO THE SEVEN LAWS OF THE CHILDREN OF NOAH

CHAIM CLORFENE and YAKOV ROGALSKY

Targum Press

First Published 1987
ISBN 0-87306-433-X

Phototypeset at Targum Press

Published by:
Targum Press Inc.
22700 W. Eleven Mile Rd.
Southfield, Mich. 48034

Distributed by:
Philipp Feldheim Inc.
200 Airport Executive Park
Spring Valley, N.Y. 10977

Feldheim Publishers Ltd.
POB 6526 Jerusalem, Israel

Printed in Israel

הרב מנחם מענדל הכהן פעלדמאן

Rabbi Mendel Feldman

5710 JONQUIL AVENUE

BALTIMORE, MD. 21215

578-9876

ב״ה

SHEARITH ISRAEL CONGREGATION

PARK HEIGHTS & GLEN AVENUES

BALTIMORE, MD. 21215

466-3060

July 28, 1986

I was privileged to review the material included
in the book, The Path of the Righteous Gentile, and
found the work to be meticulous and thoughtful.

The authors, both of whom I know to be conscientious
and God-fearing, have done a praiseworthy job.

Rabbi Mendel Feldman

With deepest gratitude to
Rav Mendel Feldman, *shlita,*
who selflessly helped guide and nurture
the development of this book.

Table of Contents

The Path of the Righteous Gentile

An Introduction to the Seven Laws
of the Children of Noah

Introduction

For the past two thousand years, Christians and Moslems and every other religious group that has had the opportunity have been proselytizing to the Jews, telling them what their religious duty should be. The Jews, by contrast, have never actively sought converts to their own religion. Perhaps this is why few people realize that Judaism, too, has something to say about what should be the religious duty of the non-Jewish peoples of the world. This book summarizes the Jewish teachings on this subject to inform and guide the Gentiles, or descendants of Noah. Jewish readers will also be interested in learning about this little-known area of Jewish study.

The doctrine of the Seven Noahide Commandments brings the Jewish idea of unity to the world. In fact, the very idea of unity in religion originated with Judaism. Whoever has this concept other than the Jews, got it from the Jews.[1] And when we speak of unity, we mean both the unity of God and the unity of mankind. The unity of God means monotheism, and the unity of mankind means a world in which all people come to God in peace and harmony.

All the religions of the world, other than Judaism, approach the idea of unity with the precept, "Believe as we believe, and the world will be one." This approach has never worked. Judaism approaches unity from an entirely different perspective. It teaches that there are two paths, not just one.[2] One path is yours. The other one is mine. You travel yours and I will travel

3

mine, and herein will be found true unity: the one God is found on both paths because the one God gave us both. The Noahide laws define the path that God gave to the non-Jewish peoples of the world.[3]

The Seven Noahide Commandments comprise the most ancient of all religious doctrines, for they were given to Adam, the First Man, on the day of his creation.[4] Wondrously, the Seven Noahide Commandments remain the newest and most uncharted of all religious doctrines. Humanity has managed to keep them new by ignoring them throughout history. But now, in these latter days when the footsteps of the Messiah can be heard by all who will listen closely, the Seven Noahide Commandments must finally be studied and observed by all the people of all the nations.

The word *commandment* is a translation of the Hebrew word *mitzvah*, which also means "connection." By observing God's commandments, a person becomes connected with God's infinite will and wisdom and thereby elicits a Godly light which shines onto his or her soul. This Godly light is eternal, and in it the soul earns eternal reward.[5] By observing the Seven Noahide Commandments, a Gentile fulfills the purpose of his creation and receives a share of the World to Come, the blessed spiritual world of the righteous.

The hurdle that must be cleared in preparation for observing the Seven Noahide Commandments is the acceptance of the idea that mankind's way to the Father is through the rabbis. Rebellion against the sanctity of rabbinic authority and tradition has been with us since those first days in the Wilderness of Sinai when the followers of Korah led a revolt against absolute rabbinic authority, as we learn in the Torah, "And they assembled themselves against Moses and against Aaron and said to them, You assume too much; for the whole of the congregation are all of them holy, and the Lord is among them; wherefore then will you lift yourselves up above the congregation of the Lord?" (Num. 16:3). In the end, God

4

performed a great miracle to demonstrate his preference for the Mosaic authority, "And the earth opened her mouth and swallowed them and their houses and all the men that were for Korah and all their wealth. And they went down, they and all who were for them, alive into the pit; and the earth closed over them and they disappeared from the midst of the congregation" (Num. 16:32,33). The lessons of the Torah are eternal as we see by all those down through the ages who have emulated the actions of Korah and his band.

When God gave the Torah to the Jewish people on Mount Sinai, the people all accepted the written Torah willingly, but God had to lift the mountain over their heads and threaten to drop it on them to persuade them to accept the Oral Torah,[6] that is, the rabbinic interpretation of the Hebrew Scriptures. If the Jews had difficulty in accepting the Oral Torah as no less divine than the scriptures themselves, how much more difficult must it be for the non-Jews. But accept the rabbis[7] they must, for the source of understanding the Seven Noahide Commandments is found in the Talmud and the later rabbinic teachings, and nowhere else.

There is a second difficulty that arises in considering the Seven Noahide Commandments. It is seemingly a semantic problem, but it has profound implications. The Gentile as well as the Jew should not relate to members of the non-Jewish nations of the world as Gentiles, but rather as Noahites. Seen as the Children of Noah, or Noahites, the non-Jewish nations of the world at once have a unique and specific spiritual role in the world, one that is exceedingly exalted. The Children of Noah are co-religionists of the Children of Israel. Together, they are peaceful partners striving to perfect the world and thereby give God satisfaction. By viewing himself as a Noahite, the Gentile becomes like the Jew, in that he is a member of a people whose peoplehood (not just his religion) is synonymous with its relationship to God.

At this time, *The Path of the Righteous Gentile* is the only book that attempts to present a framework of the doctrine of the Seven Noahide Commandments in a usable form, albeit a limited and seminal one. For reasons explained in the "Historical Overview," previous treatises on this subject were written by Jewish scholars for other Jewish scholars and were intended to remain theoretical and academic. *The Path of the Righteous Gentile* is a call to action for both the Jew and the non-Jew, the Israelite and the Noahite. As the great sage Rabbi Tarfon said: The day is short, the work is considerable, the workers are lazy, the reward is great, and the Boss is pressing.[8]

It all depends on us, which includes you. And so, this introductory book on the Seven Laws of the Children of Noah has been prepared. It is meant not as a document of final authority, but as a means by which one may become familiar with the subject.

We hope and pray that the God of Abraham, Isaac, and Israel will forgive any errors this work may contain, and that it will become an instrument for bringing all mankind closer to its Father in heaven. May His revealed Presence soon dwell among us.

Chapter One
Historical Overview

The code of Divine Law that we now know as the Seven Commandments of the Children of Noah has been with mankind since the creation of the first man, Adam. Though man is the crown of creation, he was created last. The reason that God created man last of all the creations was to serve as a perpetual lesson, symbolic of man's choice in the world. When he is fulfilling God's will, man sits atop everything that was created before him and is truly creation's crown. But when he falls in disobedience to God, he is last and lowest of all the creatures, lower even than the gnat, which consumes throughout its life but never eliminates waste, the symbol of ultimate selfishness. Even the lowly gnat follows God's will. Man alone has the option to transgress it.[1]

When God charged Adam, "And the Lord God commanded Adam, saying: Of every tree in the garden you may surely eat. But from the tree of the knowledge of good and evil you may not eat of it, for on the day that you eat of it you shall surely die" (Gen. 2:16,17), this single commandment contained the source of the Seven Noahide Commandments.[2] And more, Adam was charged by God with the responsibility of teaching the laws to future generations. The verse states that God commanded Adam, "saying." Although this word "saying" appears superfluous, it is a principle of the Torah that there are no superfluous words, for everything comes to teach us something. In this case, the word "saying" indicates that God

7

not only said the commandment to Adam, but He intended that Adam say it as well. It is a principle of Biblical analysis that when a verse states, "And the Lord spoke to Moses, saying," it means that God taught Moses something and that He expected him to teach it to the Jewish people,[3] or, as in the case of the Seven Commandments of the Children of Noah, to all of mankind.

And so, Adam taught his children the Seven Universal Laws: not to worship idols, not to curse God, not to kill, not to steal, not to engage in sexual immorality, not to eat the limb of a living animal, and to establish courts of law to enforce these laws. And so mankind developed.

The clear proof that the descendants of Adam knew these laws and were expected by the Divine Judge and Father to obey them was that 1656 years later He brought the Great Flood as a punishment for mankind's failure to keep these commandments. "And God saw the earth and, behold, it was corrupted, because all flesh had corrupted its way on the earth" (Gen. 6:12).

The classic Biblical commentary of Rashi[4] teaches that the corruption was sexual immorality and idol worship. The very next verse reads, "And God said to Noah, the end of all flesh has come before Me, because the earth is filled with wickedness" (Gen. 6:13). Rashi comments that the phrase "the earth is filled with wickedness" refers to theft. So, because of sexual immorality, idol worship, and theft (three of the seven commandments which Adam was expected to teach his children, and which mankind was expected to obey), the Creator of all destroyed all, except for the remnant, which included Noah, his wife, his three sons and their wives.

When the floodwaters settled and the earth had been wiped clean of its taint, humanity no longer had to fall back on Adam as the father of all mankind. Now mankind had a new father, Noah. And unlike Adam, who failed to fulfill God's commandments, Noah was "a righteous man, pious in his generation, and Noah walked with God" (Gen. 6:9).

And so, with a new world and a fresh start at building it in sanctity, God reaffirmed the original seven commandments that He had taught Adam. God blessed Noah and his sons and their wives and promised that He would never again destroy the world as He had done, sealing the promise for all time by striking a covenant with Noah as mankind's father as expressed in the following verses: "And God spoke to Noah and to his sons with him, saying, 'As for Me, behold, I establish My covenant with you and with your seed after you (Gen. 9:8),'" and, "And God said, 'This is the sign of the covenant that I am placing between me and your children and between all the living souls that are with you for all generations. My bow I am placing in the cloud and it shall be for a sign of the covenant between Me and the earth'" (Gen. 9:12,13).

The sign of the covenant was the rainbow, which would serve as a permanent symbol of Divine benevolence. It was the first time the rainbow had ever been seen in the world, although it had been created and readied for this moment at twilight after the sixth day of creation, between the time Adam transgressed and the Sabbath, when God rested from all He had made.[5] The rainbow with its seven colors reflected the beauty and sanctity of the Seven Commandments of the Children of Noah.

*   *   *   *

When God created Adam and placed him in the Garden of Eden, this was to be the prime dwelling place of the Divine Presence. But when Adam transgressed God's commandment, the Divine Presence withdrew and left the earth in favor of the first heaven.[6] Then, with the sin of Cain and Abel, the Divine Presence withdrew from the first to the second heaven. Then Enosh evoked idolatrous gods, and the Divine Presence went from the second to the third heaven. And from the third heaven it rose to the fourth heaven because of the Generation of the Flood.

Although Noah was righteous enough to be spared destruction and be designated the second father of mankind, despite his efforts, he failed in his attempt to effect a true rectification of Adam's sin, which was necessary to draw the Divine Presence back to Its desired residence on earth. One of the first acts he engaged in upon leaving the Ark was the planting of a vineyard (Gen. 9:20,21). Most Biblical commentaries are highly critical of this action. After all, mankind had just been destroyed. To plant a vineyard so as to grow grapes and make wine seems totally inappropriate under the circumstances. But there are those who say that Noah was attempting to rectify the sin of Adam. The Talmud states that, in one opinion, the fruit of the tree of knowledge was the grape.[7] What Adam had done was drink wine in a profane manner. It had been God's intention that Adam should wait until the Sabbath, which was to come in just a few hours, and then the fruit of the tree, the grape, would be used to sanctify the Sabbath and bear witness to the fact that God had created the world in six days and rested on the seventh.[8] It is argued that Noah knew this deeper meaning of Adam's transgression, and by planting a vineyard and using the wine for holy purposes, he could achieve the complete rectification of the sin. But Noah failed. He became intoxicated and was discovered naked by his youngest son, Ham, who shamed him by calling Noah's other two sons, Shem and Japheth, to see their father's drunken nakedness. Rashi comments on this verse (Gen. 9:22) that Ham either castrated his father or had homosexual relations with him or both. Shem and Japheth respectfully covered their father with a garment, but the damage had been done. Noah awoke and cursed Ham and his descendants, and the Divine Presence looked down in pity (Gen. 9:23-27).

The Seven Commandments of the Children of Noah remained, as before the Flood, unheeded by all but a few,

10

notably Shem and his grandson Eber, who established Houses of Study for the purpose of understanding and fulfilling the Noahide Laws.[9]

Then came the generation of the Tower of Babel. This was a generation of brilliant scientists. Not only did they learn to master many of the world's natural forces, such as controlling the weather, but they reasoned in their scientific wisdom that the earth had no Master, or, at least if it had a Master, that they were His equal, and they built a tower to the heavens to challenge the authority of God. They scientifically concluded that, since the Flood of Noah occurred in the year 1656 after creation, this meant that every 1656 years the heavens would shake, the depths would open, and the rains would come to destroy the earth.[10] And the Bible teaches, "And God descended to look at the city and the tower that the children of man had built" (Gen. 11:5). This was already from the fifth heaven.

God took measures to stop his errant children by confounding their language and scattering them to distant lands (Gen. 11:4). Originally, all of mankind spoke one language, the language of Scripture, Hebrew, the twenty-two letters of the Hebrew *alef-bet* being the very instruments of creation.[11] But now mankind had lost this merit, communicating in the seventy languages of the world.

During these times, King Nimrod arose with a wickedness that was virtually without precedent. He proclaimed himself god of all the earth and commanded all his subjects to worship him as the actual deity. Those who refused, he killed.[12]

Nimrod was called "a mighty hunter before the Lord" (Gen. 10:9). Rashi comments that the phrase "a mighty hunter" means that he captured the minds of men with his mouth and led them astray to rebel against God. "Before the Lord," Rashi says, indicates Nimrod intentionally provoked God in His Presence. Nimrod, unlike any man who had lived before him, acted wickedly in order to defy God. He knew his Master and rebelled out of spite against Him.

11

God withdrew his Divine Presence to the sixth heaven in response to the sins of Sodom and Gemorrah, primarily theft and sexual perversion. In those societies, cruelty was admired and human kindness harshly punished, often by death.[13]

The ancient Egyptians completed the job of driving God away by being wholly devoted to their many idols, more steeped in sexual perversion than the Sodomites, and by developing another form of evil to its ultimate — witchcraft.[14] With God's revealed Presence removed to the seventh and highest heaven, mankind dwelt in a world of moral and spiritual darkness.

Finally there arose a righteous man whose deeds began to draw the revealed Presence back to earth. Abraham stood alone against the world by clinging to the Creator and doing His will. He challenged Nimrod's idolatry with his belief in the One God, and eventually vanquished Nimrod completely, bringing mankind to the recognition of God and His way in the world. In Abraham's merit, the Divine Presence descended from the seventh heaven to the sixth heaven. Because of Abraham's son, Isaac, the Divine Presence descended from the sixth to the fifth heaven, then from the fifth to the fourth with Isaac's son, Jacob.

Jacob's spiritual might was awesome. He wrestled with an angel of God and defeated it (Gen. 32:25-30). Through Jacob and his children, twelve sons and one daughter, a new and distinct people on earth emerged. The Children of Israel were named after their father Jacob, who had been blessed by God and given the new name: "Your name shall no more be called Jacob, but Israel shall be your name, and He called his name, Israel" (Gen. 35:10). Rashi comments that the name Jacob implies one who comes with stealth and guile, but the name Israel denotes a prince and a ruler.

With the Children of Israel, a people of God had come into the world. Abraham, Isaac, and Israel were each mighty prophets and knew that their descendants would go down to Egypt in exile and would then be redeemed by God and given His Divine Law on Mount Sinai.

The Patriarchs fulfilled the Seven Commandments of the Children of Noah, and through their gift of prophecy saw what the Sinai Revelation would bring, and obeyed those laws as well, even though they had not been commanded concerning them. When God had blessed Isaac, it was "because Abraham listened to My voice, and kept My charge, My commandments, My statutes, and My laws" (Gen. 26:5). Rashi comments that "charge" refers to the admonitions of the Torah, which had not yet been commanded, including rabbinical prohibitions regarding the Sabbath, whereas "commandments" refers to matters such as robbery and murder (two of the Seven Noahide Commandments).[15]

In fact, there were times when a conflict over the two codes of law arose. The initial strife between Joseph and his brothers had to do with the difference between the Mosaic precept of keeping the dietary laws and the Noahide Commandment forbidding the eating of the limb of a living animal. Mosaic Law permits Jews to eat the meat of an animal that has been ritually slaughtered, even if the animal still exhibits movement in its limbs. Noahide Law does not require ritual slaughtering, but forbids Noahites to eat an animal's meat unless every trace of movement has stopped. The brothers had a heated discussion about the subject, and the sons of Leah argued that they, by following the Mosaic precept, were exempt from the Noahide prohibition. To prove the point, they slaughtered an animal according to the Mosaic precept and ate of its meat before the animal's limbs had stopped twitching. Joseph felt that they had erred in their judgment and told the matter to their father.[16] Joseph's brothers then sold him into slavery, but he had God with him and rose to become second in command in Egypt, a veritable king alongside Pharaoh. By the time he had forgiven his brothers for what they had done to him, the Divine Presence had descended from the fourth to the third heaven through the merit of Jacob's third son, Levi.

Before the Children of Israel settled in the land of Egypt,

their brother Judah had preceded them and had established a school in Goshen for the study of God's Law, both the seven commandments that they were obliged to observe and of the laws of the Torah, which they received as a heritage from Abraham, Isaac, and Israel.[17] Even during the long and bitter period of Egyptian slavery, the tribe of Levi remained in the House of Study, exempt from harsh servitude, so that the Divine Law would be remembered and understood and fulfilled.[18] And because of the righteousness of Levi's son, Kehot, whose sons were destined to carry the Holy Ark of God through the Wilderness, the Divine Presence descended from the third to the second heaven.

When Pharaoh decreed death for the male infants born to the Children of Israel, Amram, the leader of the generation and a descendant of Levi, divorced his wife, Jochebed. His idea was to stop bringing Israelite infants into the world in order to prevent their murder. Amram, as leader, knew that his action would be emulated by his people, which is precisely what happened. But his daughter, Miriam, pointed out that whereas Pharaoh had decreed only against males, Amram had decreed against all infants, male and female, by not bringing any into the world. Respecting their daughter's words, Amram and Jochebed remarried, and the child Moses was born.[19] And in Amram's merit, the Divine Presence descended from the second to the first heaven.

Moses was the most humble man who ever lived (Num. 12:3). His humility was so complete that he considered himself as nothing at all. Whatever he achieved, he saw as coming solely from God. He felt that if God had blessed another man with as many talents as he, the other man would surely have achieved more with them.[20] This self-nullification stood him in direct contrast to the self-aggrandizement of Pharaoh, who claimed to be a deity as Nimrod had.[21]

When God redeemed the Children of Israel and decimated the idolatry of the Egyptians, it was for the purpose of His

Revelation at Sinai and the Giving of the Torah. Fifty days after the Children of Israel had left Egypt, Moses ascended Mount Sinai, and in full view of 600,000 Jewish men and at least 1,400,000 women and children,[22] the Lord God of Israel descended to earth from His heavenly abode (Exod. 24:10),[23] and said "I am the Lord your God who brought you out of the land of Egypt, out of the house of bondage."

God had departed from the Garden of Eden and now had returned on Mount Sinai with the Giving of the Torah. It was a Divine Revelation of proportions that the human mind cannot even begin to comprehend. All the blind and the lame and the deaf were miraculously healed.[24] All the righteous souls who would ever be born into this world were called forth by the Lord God to witness His Divine Presence.[25] This was the seal of God, His truth.

With the Giving of the Torah, the God of Israel chose the descendants of Abraham, Isaac, and Jacob as His Chosen People, instructing them to fulfill the 613 Commandments of the Torah. He also commanded the righteous of the other nations of the world to keep the Seven Commandments of the Children of Noah and commanded Moses and his people to teach them how.[26] It was both the establishment of a new covenant and the strengthening of the old one.

The Mosaic and Noahide Laws were inextricably bound together. The Children of Noah, the righteous Gentiles, were obligated to fulfill the Seven Commandments because they were given on Mount Sinai, not because they were given to Noah. And the Children of Israel were commanded to teach the Seven Commandments to the righteous Gentiles.

When Moses ascended Mount Sinai to meet God, earth and heaven came together in a unique way. God took of His holiness and brought it to earth. For the first time in creation, physical objects could be infused with actual holiness. The Torah scroll and other writings, the sacrifices and other articles of use in the Tabernacle and Temple service, and the Children

15

of Israel themselves became holy unto the Lord, meaning separate and distinct from the rest of creation with a sanctity uniquely reserved for the service of God (Exod. 19:6).[27] This was the beginning of the true universal religion in which Israel, the Jewish people, is the priest and the Children of Noah, the righteous Gentiles, its faithful laymen.[28] The year was 2448 of the creation.[29]

During the periods when the Jewish people lived in the Holy Land, their responsibility for teaching the Gentiles the Seven Commandments was generally fulfilled. During the 410 years that the First Temple stood and the 420 years of the Second Temple, Gentiles who wanted to dwell in the Land of Israel had to agree to fulfill the Noahide Laws and had the right to enter the Holy Temple and offer sacrifices to God (Zech. 14:17-18).[30]

With respect to the nations of the world, this posed something of a problem. Influential as it was, particularly during the times of King Solomon, the Land of Israel was but one place on a rather large globe. And the observance of the Noahide Laws outside of the Land of Israel was rare. Then, in the year 4800 of creation, nearly two thousand years ago, God took a drastic step to remedy the situation. He destroyed His Holy Temple, the center of religious Jewish life, and exiled His people Israel to every corner of the planet, where they remain, for the most part, to this very day. As the Talmud states, "The Jewish people went into exile only in order to make converts, meaning to teach the nations faith in the One God."[31]

The intention was for the Jewish people to proclaim the faith in the God of their fathers and to bring all the peoples of the world into the communion of God and Israel by teaching them the Seven Commandments of Noah. But what the Jews found in the world outside their own land was a difficult situation. Mixed up with a myriad of foreign cultures, the Jews had a lifelong struggle to maintain their own traditions without being swallowed up by the cultures and traditions of the peoples around them, so as to fulfill the Biblical injunction, "Take heed

16

to yourself that you inquire not after their gods, saying: How did these nations serve their gods? Even so, I will do likewise" (Deut. 12:30). Moreover, the Jew found that people were distrustful of him and hostile, and were far too busy trying to convert him to their religions to have any time to listen to what he might have to say about the subject.

Three factors in recent times have caused a change in the situation. First, the spiritual deterioration of mankind has reached a desperate stage. Half the world follows an official doctine of atheism (which Jews consider the cruelest and most extreme form of idolatry), and much of the rest of the world is sunk into immorality and crime. Second, there exists a spirit of ecumenism, largely due to radio and television and the information explosion, in which Judaism's view concerning the non-Jew's relationship to God no longer meets with irrational responses. The third factor is that God has finally brought the appointed time, as it says, "Thus says the Lord of Hosts. In those days it shall come to pass, that ten men of all the languages of the nations shall take hold of the corner of the garment of him who is a Jew, saying, 'We will go with you, for we have heard that God is with you'" (Zech. 8:23).

Chapter Two
Knowing God

PART ONE

1. It is the foundation of foundations of all doctrines and philosophical inquiry to know that there is a First Existence (without a beginning) and that He created all existence (brought everything forth from absolute nothingness into being). And everything that is found in the heavens or on the earth exists only because of the truth of His existence.[1]

2. And if all the creatures in creation should cease to exist, He alone would still exist and in no way would He be nullified because of their nullification. For every creation needs Him, but He, Blessed Be He, does not need any of them or all of them, and His truth is not like the truth of any one of them.[2] Their existence is not imperative, but depends on His existence. Therefore, their existence is relative. But the First Existence is uncaused. His existence is absolute.

3. Of Him the prophet says, "The Lord God is truth" (Jer. 10:10). He alone is truth and there is no other truth like unto His truth.[3] And of Him the Torah says, "There is nothing else besides Him" (Deut. 4:35).

4. This Existence is the God of the universe and Master of the earth. He directs the planet with a power that has neither limit nor end, with a power that is uninterrupted, so that the planet always revolves. And it is impossible for something to revolve without there being a force causing it to revolve. And He,

Blessed Be He, causes it to revolve without a hand and without a body.[4]

5. And if it should ever occur to you that there is another deity besides Him, it is a rejection of the very Source on which everything depends.[5]

6. This God is one. He is not two or more than two, and there is no single existence that is unique and singular like His existence. He is not in a category that includes others of His species. And He is not divided into portions or sections as is a body, but His is a oneness and a uniqueness that has no equal in the universe.[6]

7. If there were many gods, they would perforce have bodies, because there is no way to differentiate one being from another except by bodily or material differences. And if the Creator had a body or any material form, He would have both a limit and an end, and His power would have a limit and an end, because it is not possible for there to be a body that has no termination point and everything pertaining to a body also has a termination point. But because of our God, Blessed Be His Name, Whose power is endless and uninterrupted, the planet revolves perpetually, for His power is not a bodily power, and because He has no body, there are no accidents or occurrences of the body that happen to Him which might divide or separate Him from another being. Therefore it is impossible for Him to be anything but One.[7]

8. If a person should think that there might be two deities, equally uncreated, what would distinguish one from the other except for their occupying different places at the same time or the same place at different times? And if you want to say that they occupy different places at the same time or the same place at different times, they are surely not limitless. Otherwise, the concept of two infinities arises, which is by definition impossible. Infinity is one and all inclusive and supremely indivisible into aspects, extremities, or forms.

9. It is explained in the Torah and the Prophets that the Holy One, Blessed Be He, has no body, for it says, "Because the Lord He is God in Heaven above and on the earth below" (Deut. 4:39), and a body cannot be in two places, and it says, "Because they saw no form" (Deut. 15), and it says, "And who is compared or equal to Me?" (Isa. 40:25), and if He had a body, He would be comparable to other bodies.[8]

10. If so, why does it say in the Torah, "And under His feet" (Exod. 24:10), and "Written by the finger of God," (Exod. 31:18), "Hand of the Lord" (Exod. 9:3), "Eyes of the Lord" (Gen. 38:7), "Ears of the Lord" (Num. 11:1) and many examples like this? All of this is because the intellect of man is unable to fathom anything other than materiality, and the Torah is given in the language of man. So all of these examples are descriptive phrases, such as, "If I whet the glitter of My sword," (Deut. 32:41). Does He have a sword? It is all only a parable. The truth is that He has no semblance or form, but all of it is the vision of the prophet, as it is written, "Can you find God by searching for Him, or can you delve into the depths of the Almighty?" (Job 11:7).[9]

11. And what was it that Moses sought when he asked God, "Please, show me Your glory" (Exod. 33:18)? Moses wished to know the truth of the existence of the Holy One, Blessed Be He, to the point where he knew it in his heart, just as one knows a person whose form is engraved in his heart, and whom he recognizes as distinct from other men. Thus did Moses yearn to know the Holy One, Blessed Be He, to the point where He would be distinct in Moses' heart like other existences, thereby knowing the truth of God's existence as it really is. And God answered him that man, while his soul is attached to a body, lacks this power of intellect and so he cannot know this truth clearly.[10]

12. Since, as it has been explained, God has no body, He is not subject to the accidents of the body. He has neither attachment

nor separation, neither place nor measurement, neither ascent nor descent, neither right nor left, neither front nor back, neither standing nor sitting, and just as He has no ending, neither has He a beginning, and He has neither life nor death as a body has, neither intellect nor wisdom like a wise man, and He neither sleeps nor wakes, and he has neither anger nor laughter, neither joy nor sadness, neither silence nor speech like the speech of man.[11]

13. And such passages in the Torah as "He sits in the heavens and laughs" (Ps. 2:4) are merely parables and similitudes, for as the sages of Israel say, the Torah was given in the language of man, and as God says, "I am the Lord, I do not change" (Mal. 3:6). If He were at times angry and at times joyous, this would surely constitute change, for all these qualities and attributes are found only in a lowly body, a physical vessel whose foundation is dust, but He, may He be blessed, is exalted far, far above any of this.[12]

PART TWO

1.   One should strive to love and fear God, Who is honored and exalted, as it says, "You should love the Lord your God" (Deut. 6:5), and "You should fear the Lord your God" (Deut. 6:13).

2.   What is the way to love Him and fear Him? When a man ponders deeply about His wondrous deeds and His manifold great creations, he will realize that God's wisdom has no equal or end, and he will immediately love and praise and glorify and desire with a great desire to know His Great Name. And when he thinks about these things, he will immediately be awestruck with fear, and he will realize that he is only a small creature, low and inconsequential, standing with extremely limited knowledge before the One Who possesses knowledge that is perfect and complete.[13]

21

PART THREE

1. "Know this day and take it unto your heart that the Lord is God in the heavens above and on the earth below, there is no other" (Deut. 4:39).

2. In the beginning, when God said, "Let there be a firmament in the midst of the waters" (Gen. 1:6), the words and letters of His blessed speech, being eternal as He is eternal, stand eternally in the firmament of the heavens as the activating life force in creation. Were God to retract His words or cause the letters of His speech to depart even for an instant, the heavens would immediately return to absolute nothingness just as they were prior to their having been created by God's saying, "Let there be a firmament."[14]

3. Thus it is with each of the Ten Utterances by which God created the world. Were the letters of God's speech to return to their Source, the entirety of creation would instantly cease to exist and would become the absolute nothingness that it was before the beginning of the six days of creation.[15]

4. One who contemplates the foregoing can begin to understand how God was one and unique and alone before He created the world, and remains equally one and unique and alone even after He created the world, and that the creation of the world in no way added anything to His completeness and perfection.[16]

5. This seems to be a paradox. How can it be that the creation of the world added nothing or effected no change in God? The seeming paradox is resolved by realizing that compared with God, Whose speech is the sole life force in creation, the world is absolutely and literally nothing and nonexistent. This is because in His Presence everything is considered nonexistent, literally null and void, and there is no place devoid of His Presence,[17] as it is written, "Do I not fill heaven and earth? saith the Lord" (Jer. 23:24).

6. When a flesh-and-blood person speaks, the words and the

22

breath of his mouth are felt and seen to leave the speaker and to be things unto themselves, but God's speech is never separated from Him, because there is no place devoid of Him and nothing outside of Him, for He is eternal and infinite.[18]

7. Even the idea of speech as applied to God is to be taken not literally but metaphorically. Just as the speech of a person reveals what was hidden in the person's thoughts, thus it is above with the Lord of Hosts, Blessed Be He, Who brought forth all of created existence from a state of hiddenness to revelation by saying the Ten Utterances as recorded in the Book of Genesis. It is this which is called speech in reference to God.[19]

8. These Ten Utterances by which the world was created are called the speech of God because through them His will went from a concealed state to a revealed state. But this so-called speech is unified with Him in absolute unity. The difference is only from the perspective of created beings, which receive their life force from God's speech, as it descends from His exalted being and creates material existence, descending level after level until it reaches this coarse physical world. Here, created beings are able to receive the Godly flow of life without losing their identities through being absorbed and nullified in their true Source, God.[20]

9. This Godly influx is concealed to avoid a revelation of God that is greater than the world can endure. Therefore, it appears to the creatures that the light and life force of the Omnipresent which is clothed in each creation, and is the true existence of each creation, is a thing apart from His Blessed Self and merely issues from Him, just as the speech of a human being issues from the person. Yet there is absolutely no concealment from the perspective of the Holy One, Blessed Be He. Nothing is obscured from Him whatsoever. To Him darkness and light are exactly the same, as it is written, "Even the darkness conceals nothing from You, but the night shines as the day" (Ps. 139:12).

10. Nor does the descent of level after level stop His blessed

speech from remaining in a state of absolute unity with Him, but it is metaphorically "like the snail whose garment is part of him."[21]

11. The error that mundane philosophers make which leads them to believe that God created the world and then abandoned it to its own devices is that they assume that the creative process of God is the same as that of man. In truth, it is far different, as it is written, "For My thoughts are not like your thoughts," and, "Thus My ways are higher than your ways" (Isa. 55:8-9). Man is merely capable of creating something from something. The human craftsman takes an ingot of silver and fashions a vessel from it. When the craftsman removes his hand from his creation, the vessel remains. This is because the craftsman merely changes the form of a created substance. However, when God created the heavens and the earth, He made them from absolute nothingness, and were He to remove His creative force, they would be as they were before He brought them forth into the state of revealed creation, that is, nonexistent.[22]

12. From the foregoing words of truth, it should be apparent how the entirety of creation is, in truth, considered null and nonexistent with respect to God's activating force and the breath of His mouth. This does not mean that the creation is an illusion. It does mean that God's Divine Force is its true existence and that creation has no independent existence of its own. For it must be remembered that the example of God's removing His original Ten Utterances was hypothetical. God has no such intention. The universe is real. It is, however, nullified to its Creator. How do we know the universe is real? Inasmuch as our limited senses and intellect are part of the created universe, the proof they offer is inconclusive. We are part of the very thing that may not exist! There is but one proof that the universe really exists. It says so in the Torah, as it is written "In the beginning, God created the heavens and the earth" (Gen. 1:1).

13. The reason that every created being and thing appears to possess an independent self-existence is that we do not grasp or see with our physical eyes the power of God and the breath of His mouth that is within creation. If permission were granted the eye to see the life force and the spirituality that flow from God to every created thing, then we would no longer see the physicality of material existence. For, since the physical world is truly nullified to its Source, if we could see the Godly source, how could we see the physical world?[23]

14. By analogy, a ray of sunlight may be seen from the earth, but from the perspective of the sun, the ray's source, all that is seen is the light that fills the sky. From the sun's perspective, the ray has no existence whatsoever.[24]

15. However, the analogy of the ray of sunlight is incomplete, because its source, the sun, exists only in one place in the heavens. The sun does not exist both in the heavens and on earth where its light appears to have a separate existence. This is in contrast to created beings, which are always within their Source, although the Source is not revealed to their eyes.[25]

16. It is not sufficient to say that God created the world during the six days of creation, for His creative activity is continuous, an infinite flow of life force. This is why it is written in the present tense, "He *creates* darkness and *forms* light,"[26] rather than in the past tense, that He *created* darkness and *formed* light. And this applies to man as well. The man who feels his own self-importance and does not recognize that the Creator is constantly bringing him forth from absolute nothingness into existence is called one whom God *created* in the past tense. This is in contrast to a person who acknowledges the truth of his existence, that it comes from God alone, constantly. This person is called one whom God *creates*.[27]

Chapter Three
Returning to God

If any one concept epitomizes the knowledge of God, it is Judaism's belief that man can achieve *complete* repentance. Judaism does not even find the word repentance sufficient, for repentance presupposes a natural state of sinfulness from which, in reality, there is no return. The Jewish idea is called *tshuvah*, return.

Christianity, for example, views man as being a hopeless victim of original sin. In that light, complete repentance is impossible. How can one return to one's pure nature if the pure nature itself is blemished?

In truth, repentance is withheld from the sinner only by his own evil mind and deceitful heart. If he sincerely wishes to draw near to God, the gate of repentance is open to him and no hindrance exists which can prevent him from attaining his goal. On the contrary, God opens the gate of righteousness for all and, in His lovingkindness and goodness, instructs man in the good way, as it is written, "Good and upright is the Lord; therefore, He will teach sinners the way" (Ps. 25:8). And it is also written, "The Lord is nigh unto all who call upon Him in truth" (Ps. 145:18).

How can the Christian idea of original sin be acceptable when nine souls have ascended to their eternal reward without experiencing death?[1] The most notable of these, of course, is the Prophet Elijah who ascended to heaven in a flaming chariot (Kings 2 2:11). Another was Serach, the daughter of Asher, who informed her grandfather Jacob that his son Joseph was alive and well in Egypt.[2] The great rabbi, the Baal ShemTov, was offered the opportunity to be the tenth to leave this earth without dying, but he chose to experience death.[3] He saw everything as emanating solely from God, therefore ultimately good and worth experiencing, as it says, "The feet of the Shechina descend even unto death" (Prov. 5:5 and 7:27).

Judaism rejects the notion of man being trapped by original sin. We learn that Abraham and Sara fulfilled what Adam and Eve failed to fulfill.[4] And Jacob, through his exalted service of God, achieved a true rectification of the sin of the Tree of Knowledge of Good and Evil.[5]

This means that man *can* return to God, no matter how far he has fallen. The method of man's return to his true and sinless state of being is systematically delineated in Judaism and workable by anyone, whether Israelite or a Noahite.

Why should man strive to return to God? The lowest reason is, of course, to avoid punishment. But there is a nobler reason. Suppose a person had in his possession a great painting by Rembrandt, for example. Not knowing it was a treasureable object, he had stored it away in the attic gathering dust and mold. Once he learns that the painting is real and that he has a masterpiece in his possession, the person will certainly go up to the attic, retrieve the painting, clean it off and restore it to its original state. Is a person's own soul not worthy of a similar honor? For it is said that of all the treasures entrusted to you by your Creator, the one most worthy of honor is your own soul.[6]

PART ONE

1. A person must realize that God, Blessed Be He, is more merciful to man than anyone or anything else can be. The Creator, Blessed Be He, does not conceal anything from a

person which might improve his personal welfare. For man is God's creation, and no one can better understand how to care for a creation than the original maker. If this principle applies to a human craftsman, who does not create any new form but merely changes the form of an already existing creation, then certainly it is true of God, Who brought man into being from absolute nothingness and sustains him at every instance and every second. God is all-knowing in the ways of what is best for man, what can damage him and what will work to his advantage.[7]

2.   One should contemplate and know that God lavishes great and abundant kindness on man. From the beginning of human existence, God has bestowed these kindnesses even without man's being worthy of them. And it is not because God has a need for man, but only because of God's great goodness and generosity.[8]

3.   One should also realize clearly that God observes him at all times and that there is nothing hidden from Him. All stand revealed before Him. God knows whether or not a person has complete trust in Him. Therefore, it is fitting that a person trust God and turn to Him, abandoning ways contrary to Him. By observing the Seven Noahide Commandments with care and deliberation, one demonstrates that he has put his complete trust in God. God will then reciprocate with trust in man, leading him to success and happiness in all matters.[9]

4.   There is no miracle in the creation as great as returning to God through repentance. Repentance is greater than wisdom. By means of wisdom, man can discriminate between good and evil, choosing the good and rejecting the evil. Nevertheless, the evil remains evil. But through repentance, man has the power to transform evil miraculously into good, for the sins themselves and the remorse over having committed them are the very actions that draw a person to God with impassioned longing and great love.[10]

28

5. A Chasidic Rebbe once happened upon a person who was a notorious sinner. The Rebbe walked up to the man and confessed that he was envious of him.

"But Rebbe," the man said, amazed, "you are a saint and I am a sinner. Why should you be envious of me?"

"Because," the Rebbe answered, "you can bring a much greater light into the world than I can. I can only bring goodness to the world by resisting sin and doing what I am supposed to do. You can transform thousands, maybe millions, of evil deeds into wondrous merits by repenting and returning to God."[11]

PART TWO

1. If a person has transgressed one or all of the Seven Noahide Commandments, either willfully or unintentionally, when he repents, he is obligated to confess verbally, specifying his sins before the God of kindness, Blessed Be He. How should he confess? He should speak words to this effect: "I beseech you, God, I have sinned unintentionally (or "I have transgressed willingly"). I have acted out of spite before You and I have done such-and-such. I regret my actions and am ashamed of them and will not do such-and-such again." This is the essence of confession. Anyone who increases the content of his confession and elaborates upon it is praiseworthy.[12]

2. A punishment imposed on a person by a Noahide court of law serves as an atonement for the transgression if the person confesses his sins to God in the above manner. Similarly, if one injures a friend or causes him monetary loss, even if he has paid back what he owes, he has not atoned for his transgression until he confesses to God and resolves never to repeat such a deed again.

3. Repentance atones for all sins. Even if one is evil all the

days of his life and returns to God on the last of his days, none of his wickedness is mentioned to him in the Divine Judgment.[13]

4.   What is complete repentance? If, after having confessed, it occurs to the person to repeat the transgression done in the past, and if the opportunity to do it arises, and if he resists and refrains from doing it solely because of his repentance and not because of his fear of anyone (a policeman, for instance), and not because he is too weak physically and can no longer do it, then he has achieved complete repentance.

For example, if a man has had a forbidden relationship with a woman and he has repented and confessed, and after a time it happens that he finds himself alone with her again, and now he resists and does not transgress, this is a person who has done complete repentance.[14]

5.   If a person returns to God (repenting of his transgressions) only in his old age, at a time of life when he is no longer able to repeat the transgressions of the past, although this is not the highest form of repentance, it does help the person and he is considered a true penitent who has returned to God.

6.   Even if one transgresses all his life and repents the day of his death and dies a penitent, all his sins are forgiven. Thus, if one remembers his Creator and returns to Him before he dies, he is forgiven.

7.   And what is repentance? It is when the sinner abandons his sin, removing it from his thoughts, and is completely resolved not to do it again. Consequently, he regrets what has happened in the past and accepts God, the Knower of secrets, as his witness that he will never return to such a sin again. And he needs to confess verbally and state the resolutions that he made in his heart.[15]

8.   One who confesses with words and does not resolve in his heart to leave his sin is like one who immerses in a ritual pool while grasping a dead rat in his hand. The immersion in the pool brings no purification until he discards the unclean object.[16]

9. On the path of repentance, the penitent should cry to God with tears and supplications and should give charity according to his capability, at least ten percent of his income and preferably twenty percent. He should also distance himself from the thing in which he sinned or the person with whom he sinned. He should change all his deeds and tread a straight path, and he should exile himself from his present residence since exile is an atonement because it brings a person to humility, and the essence of repentance comes through a broken heart and a humble spirit.[17]

10. It is praiseworthy for the penitent to confess publicly, even to the extent of informing others of his transgressions, saying to his peers, "I have sinned against so-and-so and I have done such-and-such. But I have changed my ways, and I deeply regret my past."[18]

11. One who is haughty and does not inform others of his transgressions, choosing rather to conceal them, does not do complete repentance.

12. Public declaration refers to the sins between oneself and his fellow man. The sins that are between oneself and his Creator need not be broadcast, and, in truth, it is considered the ultimate of brazenness to reveal them, as it shows that the person is not embarrassed about them. Let him simply return to God, Blessed Be He, specifying his sins before Him. Any public confession should be in a general way without specifying actions, and he should consider it a blessing that his iniquity has not become revealed.

13. Repentance helps only with sins that one commits between himself and God. For sins that are between oneself and his fellow man, he has to pacify his fellow and ask forgiveness from him.[19]

14. If a person receives an apology, he should never refuse to be pacified, but should forgive easily and be slow to feel anger toward another. At the time someone asks forgiveness of him,

he should grant favor with a full heart and a sincere spirit.[20]

15. Every person should consider himself perfectly balanced between reward and punishment. Similarly, he should see the entire world as similarly balanced because of his deeds. If he commits one sin, he tilts the scales of judgment for himself and for the entire world toward guilt and condemnation, and consequently he can be the cause of the whole world's destruction. But if he does one good deed, he can tilt the scales of judgment for himself and the whole world toward merit and can bring salvation and deliverance for himself and the whole world.[21]

PART THREE

1. The power of self-determination is given to every person. If he wants to direct himself toward good and righteousness, the power is in his hand; if he wants to direct himself to the way of evil, the power is similarly his.[22]

2. Man is unique in this world, and there is not another creation that can compare to him in this regard. Man is intellectually aware of good and evil. He does what he wishes to do, and no one can prevent him from choosing to do good or evil.

3. One should banish the idea that fools speak about, that God has decreed man's destiny from birth whether he will be righteous or wicked. There is no such thing. Every person has the ability to become righteous or wicked, compassionate or cruel, generous or selfish. And so it is with all other character traits and abilities to live within the normative conduct set for man by the commandments of God.[23]

It is true, however, that the individual may be born with tendencies toward specific problematic behavior, but at all times it is within his power to overcome these natural tendencies. No one is born a thief or a sexual deviant.[24]

4. If God had predetermined the individual's destiny, whether for good or for evil, on what basis could the righteous be rewarded and the wicked be punished? Just as the Creator desired that fire and wind should naturally rise upward, and water and earth should naturally descend, and that a planet should move in a circular motion, and all other creatures of the world should act in accord with the nature that God chose for them, thus did God desire that man should have the free will to determine his actions.[25]

5. Therefore, man is judged according to his deeds. If he does good, good is done to him. If he does evil, evil is repaid him. And at a future time, he must surrender himself to Judgment for his thoughts, speech, and actions. If a person fulfills the Seven Noahide Commandments, thereby doing good in this world, he is repaid with boundless good from God.

6. The reward for doing good is hundreds of times greater than the punishment for doing evil, for it is written, "for I the Lord thy God am a jealous God, visiting the iniquity of the fathers upon the children unto the third and fourth generation of them that hate Me; and showing mercy unto the thousandth generation of them that love Me" (Exod. 20:5-6).

PART FOUR

1. Whenever a person commits a transgression with his own knowledge and will, it is proper that he be punished for it so that he be paid for his deeds. God knows exactly how he should be paid. The judgment may be that the sinner should be punished in this world with afflictions of his body (various diseases or seeming accidents). Or the punishment might take the form of loss of property and wealth, or the sinner's children might be afflicted because of his wrongdoings. Also, there are

sins that are judged to be repaid in the World to Come, and so no harm befalls the transgressor in this world. And there are sins that must be paid for both in this world and in the World to Come.[26]

2. One should consider it a great kindness to be punished in this world, because the World to Come is eternal and everything of it is eternal. This reveals a glimmer of understanding of why the righteous suffer and the wicked prosper. It is as if God says of the wicked, "The little good he did in this world I will repay him in this world so that there remains no reward for him in the Eternal World, and the payment for his sins awaits him in fullest measure." And of the righteous, it is as if God says, "For his few sins I will punish him in this world, where afflictions are transitory, and for his great number of merits I will withhold reward in this world so that I can bestow upon him the greatest possible measure of eternal good in the World to Come."

3. When we speak of a man paying for his wicked deeds, this presumes that he does not repent and abandon them. But if he repents, it is considered a shield between him and the punishment. And just as a man sins because of his own understanding and free will, he can also repent through his own understanding and free will.[27]

4. There is a circumstance in which God does not offer a person the opportunity to repent. When with his own understanding and free will, a person commits an extremely grave sin or an overwhelming number of sins (such as causing many others to sin by leading them to idolatry or causing them to follow a false religious doctrine), the opportunity to abandon his evil is not granted to him in order that he should be lost in the sins that he committed. However, this merely means that repentance is not made easy for the person. Nevertheless, it is written that nothing can stand between a man and repentance, for a person can always overcome the obstacles and through strength of will return to God in full repentance.[28]

5. A person should constantly regard himself as being close to death, and finding himself standing in sin, he should immediately repent from all his sins. He should not say, "When I grow older, I will repent." Perhaps he will die before he reaches old age.[29]

6. One should not say that repentance applies only to sins involving actual deeds, such as forbidden sexual relations and theft. For just as a man must repent of those, he must become introspective concerning his evil characteristics and repent of them, from his anger and his hatred and from jealousy and folly and from pursuit of wealth and honor and excessive gluttony and other base character traits. From all of them, he must return to God. For a person who is sunk into these base pursuits and evil traits, it is harder to abandon graver sins involving actual evil deeds.[30]

7. A true penitent should not worry that, as a result of his sins, he is a long way from the exalted status of the righteous. The truth is that he is loved and treasured by the Creator as if he had never committed a sin. Moreover, when he repents, his reward is enormous: he has tasted sin and departed from it, and has conquered his evil inclination. This makes him far greater than one who has never tasted sin, for he has achieved a greater spiritual conquest.[31]

8. The ways of the penitent should be humble and extremely modest. If fools and boors taunt him about his previous deeds and say to him, "Yesterday you were doing such-and-such, and now look at you trying to be so high and mighty," he should pay no attention to them, but listen silently and rejoice and know that their insults are bringing him great merit. When a penitent is embarrassed about his past deeds and is humiliated because of them, his merits are increased and his spiritual level is exalted.[32]

9. It is a grave sin to say to a penitent, "Remember your previous deeds," or to mention anything of his past ways in

35

order to embarrass him, or to mention ideas or incidents that will remind him of what he has done.

10. Great is repentance, for it draws a person close to God, and the further one's distance, the closer and more beloved one can become through repentance. "Yesterday he was despicable in front of God; he was disgusting, distanced, and an abomination. And today, he is precious, close, and beloved."[33]

PART FIVE

1. The treasure reserved for the righteous is eternal life in the World to Come. This is a life that does not incorporate death. It is a good that does not coexist with evil. And the punishment for the wicked is that they do not merit this life, but they will be cut off and will die out. And all who do not merit this life are truly considered dead. The wicked are cut off in their wickedness and perish like animals. That is to say that the wicked one whose soul is severed from the body by spiritual extinction does not merit the eternal life of the World to Come.[34]

2. Loss of the life of the World to Come is the most terrible retribution, for this is a total loss and a complete destruction. It is a loss than can never be regained because repentance and return to God can be achieved only while the soul is in the body in this material world. Once the soul has separated from the body, it is no longer the time for good deeds or wicked deeds or repentance. Then it is the time for reward or punishment.[35]

3. There are certain misguided people who imagine that the reward for obeying God's commandments and for following the way of truth is to inherit a paradise where they are able to eat and drink sumptuous foods and beverages, to enjoy relationships with "beautiful forms," to wear linen and brocaded garments, to dwell in ivory palaces and use vessels of gold and silver, and other similar fantasies. The intelligent among

mankind will easily see that these images are foolish and vain, and that there is neither inner purpose nor spiritual meaning to them. These ideas betray a lack of understanding and a compulsion for materialism, for it is only because we have physical bodies that these things have any meaning. All of these dreams of sensory delights are attractive only to the body; the soul has no longing for them. The soul desires to fulfill bodily needs only so as to establish and maintain health, and takes no pleasure in physical delights at all.[36]

4. In the time of the eternal life where there is no body nor any physical existence at all, these material things will be entirely nullified. And there, in the World to Come, the great goodness is for the soul alone. And there is no way in this world to grasp or comprehend any understanding of this pleasure whatsoever. But the delights of the World to Come are glorious beyond human concept, and there is nothing of this world to compare to their supernal goodness.

5. The sages of Israel call it the World to Come not because it will exist in a future time and cannot be found here and now, but because it is the life that comes to man after the physical life of this world, in which the soul is encased in a physical body. The World to Come exists now and can be found now. It is found as it has been found from the very beginning.[37]

6. We are commanded to walk the middle path for it is the good and proper way, as it says, "You should walk in His ways" (Deut. 30:16). Just as God is called gracious, man must be gracious. Just as God is called merciful, man must be merciful. Man is obligated to follow the ways of God to the fullest extent of his ability.[38]

7. A person can accustom himself to this manner of conduct by performing deeds that reflect moderation, repeating them constantly until they become ingrained and established traits. And because these traits are called names such as gracious, merciful, kind, righteous, which the Creator is called, this way

of the Middle Path is called the way of God. Whoever walks this path brings goodness and blessing to himself.[39]

8. This middle path is a striving for moderation in all things, in physical pleasures, emotional expression, even intellectual and spiritual pursuits. A parable is given of a religious man who discovers that by withdrawing from a certain physical pleasure, he automatically feels closer to God. So what does he do? He acts in the extreme, becoming a hermit, denying himself everything of this world, denying himself anything of human existence. It does not take long before he degenerates to a level of inhumanity like a wild animal, further from God than when he began his spiritual journey. We can understand the cause of his failure by considering two men, one with a gold coin and the other with a million gold coins. Obviously, the man with a million gold coins has 999,999 more than the man with one. Now consider the case of three men, one with one gold coin, a second with a million gold coins, and a third with infinite gold coins. Who is closer to the one with infinite gold coins, the man with one or the man with a million? They are both exactly the same distance away. So it is with any field of human endeavor. Man is a finite being with limited intellect, limited emotions, limited physical strength. God is infinite. There is no way that man, by using his own reason and power, can approach the Creator. This is why the hermit's conclusion, logical as it may have seemed, failed him. Man can approach the Infinite only by following the method prescribed for him by the Infinite, and the method prescribed is the way of moderation, the middle path.

9. There are exceptions. When it comes to anger or false pride, one should strive to avoid these destructive traits to the ultimate. Anger is controlled and ultimately eliminated by speaking softly to all people at all times and in all situations.[40] And pride is circumvented by realizing that one is nothing and achieves nothing except for what God bestows as a gift. Another

exception to clinging to the middle path is what is called *shtus d'kedusha*, the foolishness of holiness. This means that man, finding himself in a situation of being sunk in the pursuit of physical pleasures, even permissible physical pleasures, must sometimes act in the extreme to counter the situation and eventually achieve moderation.[41]

10. In order to assure success in one's strivings, it is important to select a respected friend as both a consultant and a confidant. When matters of doubt or concern arise pertaining to performance of the Seven Laws of Noah, another's assessment of the situation will provide objectivity in determining the appropriate course of action. This is called, *Aseh lecha rav* (attain a teacher for yourself).[42] This spiritual "buddy system" will expand one's perspective and clarity, objectives that can be met even if the advisor is less than a towering genius or spiritual giant. What is desired here is the ability to open up in a sincere dialogue. This can be achieved even with an advisor who is on a lower level than the one seeking advice.

11. Every person on the earth whose spirit is humble and who differentiates between good and evil in order to be able to stand before God, to serve Him and know Him and walk upright in His path, removing the yoke of the scheming and calculating with which most people conduct their lives, sanctifies the Holy of Holies. God will be this person's portion and inheritance in this world and the World to Come forever and ever. And he will merit success in all his material efforts in this world.[43] As it is written, "Seek the Lord while He may be found; call upon Him while He is near" (Isa. 55:6).

Chapter Four

The Seven Laws of the Children of Noah

1. With respect to God's commandments, all of humanity is divided into two general classifications: the Children of Israel and the Children of Noah.

2. The Children of Israel are the Jews, the descendants of the Patriarch Jacob. They are commanded to fulfill the 613 Commandments of the Torah.

3. The Children of Noah comprise the seventy original nations of the world and their branches. They are commanded concerning the Seven Universal Laws, also known as the Seven Laws of the Children of Noah or the Seven Noahide Laws.[1] These Seven Universal Laws pertain to idolatry, blasphemy, murder, theft, sexual relations, eating the limb of a living animal, and establishing courts of law.

4. All Seven Universal Laws are prohibitions. Do not wonder at this. Negative commandments are of a higher order than positive commandments, and their fulfillment, which takes more effort than positive commandments, earns a greater reward.

5. Men and women are equal in their responsibility to observe the seven commandments.[2]

6. It is a matter of dispute as to when a person becomes responsible for his or her actions under these laws. One opinion holds that it depends on the intellectual development of the individual.[3] According to this opinion, as soon as a child has attained the maturity to understand the meaning and signif-

40

icance of the Seven Universal Laws, he is obligated to the fullest extent of the law. The other opinion is that a boy reaches the age of legal responsibility at his thirteenth birthday and a girl at her twelfth birthday.[4]

7. The Children of Noah are permanently warned concerning the Seven Universal Laws. This means that ignorance of the law is not a valid defense. One cannot claim, for example, that he did not know that idolatry was one of the seven commandments. Nor can he claim that he did not know that bowing down to an idol constitutes idolatry. (He can, however, claim that he did not know that such-and-such was an idol, for this is not ignorance of the law.) Therefore, one is duty bound to study the Seven Universal Laws to the best of one's ability and to teach the knowledge of them to one's children.

8. When one of the Children of Noah resolves to fulfill the Seven Universal Commandments, his or her soul is elevated. This person becomes one of the *Chasidei Umot ha-Olam,* the Pious Ones of the Nations, and receives a share of the Eternal World.[5] The Holy Scriptures call one who accepts the yoke of fulfilling the Seven Universal Laws a *ger toshav,* a proselyte of the gate. This person is permitted to live in the Land of Israel and to enter the Holy Temple in Jerusalem and to offer sacrifices to the God of Israel.[6]

9. Although the Children of Noah are commanded only concerning the Seven Universal Commandments, they are permitted to observe any of the 613 Commandments of the Torah for the sake of receiving divine reward.[7] The exceptions to this are:[8]

    a. Observing the Sabbath in the manner of the Jews (resting from the actions that were needed for the building of the Tabernacle during the Exodus from Egypt)

    b. Observing the Jewish holy days in the manner of the Jews (resting in a similar manner to the Sabbath)

   c.   Studying those parts of the Torah that do not apply to the Noahites' service of God

   d.   Writing a Torah scroll (the Five Books of Moses) or receiving an *aliyah* to the Torah (reading a portion of the Torah at a public gathering)

   e.   Making, writing, or wearing *tefillin*, the phylacteries worn during prayer that contain portions of the Torah

   f.   Writing or affixing a *mezuzah*, the parchment containing portions of the Torah, to one's doorposts or gateposts

(Note: A prime purpose of the Seven Universal Laws is to teach the Children of Noah about the Oneness of God, and therefore those parts of Torah that pertain to this knowledge are permissible for him to study. This includes the entirety of the twenty-four books of the Hebrew Scriptures. Also, the study of any part of the Torah that brings one to greater knowledge concerning the performance of the Seven Noahide Commandments is permissible. But Talmudic or Halakhic study of subjects that pertain exclusively to the Jew's service of God is forbidden. The Noahite who studies portions of the Torah that do not pertain to him damages his soul.[9])

10. If a Noahite is striving in the learning of Torah or keeping the Sabbath in the manner of Jews or reveals new aspects of Torah, he may be physically restrained and informed that he is liable for capital punishment, but is not put to death.

(Note: The action taken against him is only meant to dissuade him from doing forbidden acts. If the court that is established in consonance with the Seven Universal Laws gives the death penalty to a Noahite, the execution is an atonement for this person's transgression, and consequently one who transgresses and is punished by the court can merit a portion in the World to Come.[10] Furthermore, the Noahite must experience reincarnation to be able to atone for transgressions he had done.)

11. The responsibility of The Seven Noahide Laws is a yoke of faith in God. This means that the laws must be observed solely because God commanded them. If the Children of Noah observe these Seven Universal Laws for any reason or intention other than to fulfill God's will, the performance is invalid and no divine reward is received. This means that if one of the Children of Noah says, "These laws seem sensible and beneficial, therefore I will observe them," his actions accomplish nothing and he receives no reward.[11]

12. When one of the Children of Noah engages in the study of the Seven Universal Laws, he is able to attain a spiritual level higher than the High Priest of the Jews, who alone has the sanctity to enter the Holy of Holies in the Temple in Jerusalem.[12]

13. If one of the Children of Noah wishes to accept the full responsibility of the Torah and the 613 Commandments, he or she can convert and become a Jew in every respect. One who elects to do this is called a *ger tzedek*, a righteous proselyte.[13] It is a principle of Judaism, however, not to seek converts, and one who requests conversion is generally discouraged. Should the person persist in the desire to convert, counsel should be taken only with an Orthodox rabbi or scholar, for conversion not in accord with *Halakha*, Torah Law, is no conversion at all, and conversion supervised and bestowed by rabbis who themselves do not follow the laws of the Torah are null and void, neither recognized in heaven nor by any God-fearing Jew.

14. It is incorrect to think that since the Children of Israel have 613 Commandments and the Children of Noah have seven commandments, the ratio of spiritual worth is proportionally 613 to seven. The truth is that the Seven Universal Laws are general commandments, each containing many parts and details, whereas the 613 Commandments of the Torah are specific, each relating to one basic detail of the Divine Law. Therefore, the numerical disparity in no way reflects the relative spiritual worth of the two systems of commandments.[14] The

prime difference in the service of the Israelite and that of the Noahite is that the Noahite sees the existence of existence, that is, he refines the world, whereas the Israelite sees the non-existence of existence, that is, he reveals the Godliness in the world. Of course, refining the world reveals its inherent Godliness and revealing Godliness automatically refines the world.

15. The statutory punishment for transgressing any one of the Seven Laws of Noah is capital punishment.[15] According to some, punishment is the same whether one transgresses with knowledge of the law or is ignorant of the law.[16] According to others, a transgressor of the Noahide Law who is ignorant of the law receives the death penalty only in the case of murder.[17]

16. If the courts cannot punish an individual for lack of witnesses or any other reason (see the chapter on Courts of Law), the transgressor will be punished by Divine Decree.[18]

17. Besides the Seven Universal Commandments, the Children of Noah have traditionally taken it upon themselves to fulfill the commandment of honoring father and mother.[19] (see the chapter on Honoring Father and Mother).

18. Some authorities are of the opinion that the Children of Noah are obligated to fulfill the commandment of giving charity.[20] Others state that it is proper and meritorious for the Children of Noah to give charity but that it is not actually commanded of them.[21]

19. If a Noahite who follows the Seven Universal Laws gives charity, the Israelites accept it from him and give it to the poor of Israel, since through the merit of giving charity to the poor among the Jewish people one is given life by God and saved from death. But a Noahite who does not accept the yoke of the Seven Noahide Laws and gives charity is not permitted to give it to the needy of Israel. His charity may be given to poor Noahites only.

20. If one of the Children of Noah arises and performs a miracle and says that God sent him, then instructs others to add to or subtract from any of the Seven Universal Laws or explains them in a way not heard at Mount Sinai, or claims that the 613 Commandments given to the Jews are not eternal, but limited to a fixed period of time, this person is deemed a false prophet and incurs the death penalty.[22]

21. There is an oral tradition that the Children of Noah are forbidden to interbreed animals of different species or to graft trees of different kinds,[23] although some authorities hold that they are permitted to do either.[24] However, they may wear *shaatnez* (clothing containing both wool and linen) and they may plant different seeds such as grape and wheat in the same field, which are acts forbidden to Jews.[25] Forbidden interbreeding and grafting are not punishable in courts of law.

22. The Sages of Israel state that Children of Ketura (the sons of Abraham's concubine, Hagar) who were born after Ishmael and Isaac must by law be circumcised. Since today the descendants of Ishmael are intermixed with the descendants of the other sons of Hagar, all are obligated to be circumcised on the eighth day after they are born. Those transgressing this are not liable for the death penalty.[26] This law applies only to Semitic peoples, although all other nations are allowed to circumcise if they desire.

23. One opinion holds that only the six sons of Hagar and not their descendants were obligated to be circumcised.[27]

24. In accord with the Seven Universal Commandments, man is enjoined against creating any religion based on his own intellect. He either develops religion based on these Divine Laws or becomes a righteous proselyte, a Jew, and accepts all 613 commandments of the Torah.[28]

(Note: Concerning making holidays for themselves, Noahites may participate in the celebration of certain Jewish holidays, such as Shavuot, celebrating the Giving of the Torah, since the Children of Noah received their commandments at the same time, or Rosh Hashanah, the Jewish New Year and Day of Judgment, since all mankind is judged by God on that day, so it should therefore be important to the Noahite as well as the Israelite. Rosh Hashanah is also the day that Adam, the First Man, was created by God, and all mankind is descended from Adam just as it is from Noah.[29] Even these, however, the Noahite celebrates only in order to bring additional merit and reward to himself, and he may not rest in the manner of the Jews. Moreover, the Noahite is strictly forbidden to create a new holiday that has religious significance and claim that it is part of his own religion, even if the religion is the observance of the Seven Noahide Laws. For example, it would be forbidden to make a holiday celebrating the subsiding of the waters of the Flood of Noah or anything of the like. And, all the more so, it would be forbidden to institute holidays that ascribe religious significance to events outside the purview of the Seven Noahide Commandments. Celebrating secular activities and commemorating historical events, even if they involve a festive meal, are permissible.)

25. The nations of the world acknowledge the existence of God and they do not transgress the will of God. Their failing is an inability to be nullified to God, and they deny His Oneness by thinking that they themselves are separate entities, calling Him the God of gods. Therefore, we find that when they transgress the Seven Noahide Commandments, it is only because the spirit of folly enters them and covers the truth, concealing it from them.[30] But from their essential being, they are not able to transgress the Will of God. Therefore, even Balaam, the wicked prophet who had sexual relations with an animal, his ass, which is a clear transgression of the Seven Noahide Laws, said, "I am not able to transgress the word of God" (Num. 22:18).

26. The commandment to be fruitful and multiply was given to

Noah, but inasmuch as it was not repeated at Mount Sinai, this commandment is not considered part of the Seven Universal Laws.[31] However, the Children of Noah have the obligation to make the whole earth a dwelling place for mankind.[32] This is minimally achieved by every couple giving birth to a male and a female child who are in turn capable of reproduction.[33] Moreover, the couple that bears more children is credited with bringing more spiritual goodness into the world, assuming that these children are reared in an environment of morality by fulfilling the Seven Universal Laws.

27. A Noahite who strikes an Israelite causing even a slight wound, though he is theoretically condemned for this, does not receive the death penalty.[34]

28. When a Noahite dies, he is to be buried in the earth, "for out of it were you taken; for you are dust and unto dust you shall return" (Gen. 3:19). This does not mean that the Children of Noah transgress one of the Seven Commandments by utilizing another process such as cremation or cryogenic preservation, but they will lack the atonement that burial in the earth accomplishes.[35]

29. By observing the Seven Universal Laws, mankind is given the means by which it can perfect itself. The individual, through these laws, has the power to refine his essential being, and can reach higher and higher without limit. For it is written, "I call heaven and earth to bear witness, that any individual, man or woman, Jew or Gentile, freeman or slave, can have the Holy Spirit bestowed upon him. It all depends on his deeds."[36] And it is also written, "Ultimately, all is understood: fear God and observe His commandments, for this is the completion of man" (Eccles. 12:13).

Chapter Five
Idolatry

PART ONE

1.   The essence of the Seven Universal Laws is the prohibition against idolatry.   One who worships another deity besides the Creator denies the essence of religion and rejects the entirety of the Seven Universal Laws.   But one who guards himself against idolatry demonstrates belief in God and affirms the entirety of the Seven Universal Laws.[1]

2.   The commandment prohibiting idolatry teaches that one should serve no created thing — no angel, no plant, no star, nothing of the four fundamentals, earth, water, fire, and air, nor anything that is formulated from them.   Even if the worshiper knows that God is the Supreme Being and worships creation as a way of glorifying God's greatness and His ability to create great beings and things, nevertheless this is idol worship.[2]

3.   A person may ponder the heavenly spheres and observe that they do not die like other things and that it is therefore proper to bow down to them and serve them.   To do this is to place them between oneself and the Creator.   For although God may have assigned these celestial beings certain roles in the conduct of the world, nevertheless, man's responsibilities are to God and not to God's messengers.   This, in fact, is how idolatry came to exist in the world.   The generations that lived immediately after Adam recognized that God had created magnificent heavenly beings, the sun to rule by day and the moon to rule by night.

And these people began to honor God's exalted messengers. Soon it was forgotten that these messengers had been appointed by the Creator, and the sun and the moon began to be honored for their own greatness. This devolved to the worship of these creations as deities themselves without awareness of the God that had created them.[3]

4. Although there are opinions which state that the Children of Noah transgress the prohibition of idolatry from the moment they make an idol, the final law is that the transgression does not come into effect until a person actually worships or serves the idol.[4]

5. According to many authorities, a Noahite is not warned about the concept of "partnership with God."[5] The concept of partnership is the acknowledgment of the existence of the God of Israel in combination with the belief in the possibility and existence of a deity (independent will) other than God. So long as ascribing power to a deity other than the Creator remains conceptual, it is permissible to the Children of Noah according to many authorities. But worship of this independent being is clearly idolatry. The danger of the concept of partnership is that it frees people to act in accord with nonexistent gods and opens a doorway to actual idolatry. Most recent authorities agree that Children of Noah are forbidden to believe in a partnership.[6] But even according to these, the Children of Noah are permitted to swear by the name of an idol in combination with God (to swear by the Lord of Hosts and a Hindu deity, for example).

6. The Children of Noah are not commanded to sanctify God's Name by refusing to bow to an idol in the face of a threat to their lives.[7] And there is a dispute whether the Children of Noah are even allowed to choose to lay down their lives in this manner, since they are not commanded to do so.[8] However, since the Children of Noah may perform any of the 613 Commandments of the Torah to receive reward (with the notable exceptions found in the previous chapter), then it would

follow that the Noahite may choose to lay down his life for the sanctification of God's name rather than bow to an idol, even though not commanded to do so.

7. Many books have been written by idol worshipers concerning the nature of their idolatry, the service, procedures, and laws. One should not read these books at all, nor should one think about them nor speak of them. Even studying the formation of an idolatrous figure or asking how something is served without having the intention of serving it might cause one to be led to engage in idolatrous practices.[9]

8. Anyone who acknowledges that an idolatrous religion is true, even though he does not serve the idol, reviles the mighty and exalted Name of God.[10]

PART TWO

1. Many different types of idolatrous service exist and the service for one idol is not like the service of another.[11] For example, the idol Peor was served by man's defecating before it. (Note: This came about in a degenerative way, similar to the growth of idolatry itself. Original worshipers of this idol attained such a state of ecstasy that they lost control of themselves and defecated. Their children saw the effect and, misunderstanding the cause, concluded that the worship was defecation. The lesson from this is still important today. That it "feels good" is no proof of a religion's truth or validity.)

2. A person transgresses only when he worships the idol in the normal manner ascribed to each respective idol. Consequently, courts of law have to know the appropriate service for the idol in any case of idolatry.

3. The preceding law applies to unique forms of worship. If, however, the person bows down or offers sacrifices or incense or a libation (the four forms of service of the Holy Temple in

Jerusalem) to any one of the idols, he incurs the death penalty even though this may not be the way of official worship.[12]

4. Food placed upon an altar as an offering to an idol is forbidden to be eaten.[13] There is a difference of opinion concerning foods unlikely to be offered to an idol, such as a grasshopper or a cockroach.[14]

5. Things such as water and salt, which are not normally in the category of offerings to an idol, are forbidden if they are found directly in front of an idol or within the curtains that surround the idol.

6. It is forbidden to honor an idol even by offering things to it outside the boundaries that surround the idol. This is considered decorating the idol. (Throwing coins at an idol or even into a pool of water by an idol, such as the oriental gods and demigods commonly seen today, would seem to be in the category of honoring an idol and symbolically ascribing powers to it. Otherwise, why throw the money, which is clearly an act of beseeching a power for returned good fortune?)

7. If something has been prepared to be offered to an idol, but has not yet been offered, it is permitted for personal use. One should be strict, however, and not use anything found in the house of idol worship. Therefore, one should never take candles from the place of idol worship.[15]

(Note: One should not purchase or use the sticks of incense sold by any of the idolatrous religions or pseudoreligious groups. For example, as most Hindu sects are pantheistic and idolatrous, incense and health foods purchased from such groups are questionable, for the foods themselves are likely to have been worshiped. In truth, any religious food discipline wherein the foods themselves or the combinations of the foods themselves are honored as curatives or wondrous in their health-giving properties may be idolatrous. Concerning the verse, "Man does not live by bread alone, but by every word that proceeds from the mouth of God" (Deut. 8:3), we are

51

taught that it is not the bread itself which nurtures the body of man and gives it strength but the Word of God, which is enclothed in the bread and gives the bread its existence.[16] These letters "the word that proceeds from the mouth of God," not only give the bread its existence, but when ingested by man, nurture his physical body. Obviously the same is true of any food or herb or wonder drug that heals, it is merely the power of God within that food or herb or wonder drug that is the healing agent.)

8. If one offers an idol excrement or pours it a libation of urine, he transgresses, as this falls in the category of sprinkling, one of the four services in the Holy Temple in Jerusalem.[17]

9. If someone slaughters an animal that is missing one of its limbs, he is held harmless unless such is this idol's particular service.

10. If a man lifts a brick and says to it, "You are my god," and any such similar speech, he is liable for idolatry. Even if he would retract immediately and say, "This is not my god," his retraction is of no help. This does not mean that the person cannot repent. He surely can repent and God will forgive his idolatry. But if his speech was witnessed, he will be brought to trial and condemned as an idolator notwithstanding his retraction or his repentance. Repentance is good only between man and God. Jurists and courts of law lack the power to search a man's heart to determine the sincerity of his repentance. This only God can do.[18]

11. One who worships an idol according to the prescribed ritual, even if he does it contemptuously, is liable. For example, if one defecates in front of Peor in order to disgrace the idol, since he performs the prescribed worship, he is liable.[19]

12. So long as a person accepts the idol as god, even if he worships it only because its workmanship is stunningly beautiful or because he fears that some evil will otherwise befall him, he is liable.[20]

13. If a person serves an idol in the manner of one of the four forms of service used in the Holy Temple in Jerusalem — prostrating, sacrificing, sprinkling sacrificial blood, pouring libations — and serves the idol with love and fear, but without accepting it as a god, he is held harmless. If he hugs it or kisses it or dusts it off or pours water on it to cleanse the dust off or anoints it or clothes it or does other things in order to honor it, these are in the category of prostrating oneself to it.

14. If a thorn gets stuck in a person's foot while he is in front of an idol, he should not bend down to remove it, as it appears he is bowing down to the idol. This holds true even if there is no one around to observe the act. This is also true if he drops his money in front of the idol and wishes to pick it up. Rather, the person should first sit, then remove the thorn or pick up the money.[21] Or he should turn his back to the idol or turn aside from it before removing the thorn or picking up the money. And if for any reason a person has to remove his hat for a personal need, he should not remove it until he passes before the idol so that it does not appear as if he is removing it to pay respects to the idol.

(Note: There is an idolatrous group in Jerusalem that brings tourists to its house of worship. The door leading to the room where the idol is kept is extremely low so that anyone entering the room has to bend down to enter, thus forcing each tourist who enters to appear as if he or she were bowing to the idol.)

15. If there is statuary with faces that draw in or pour out water from the mouth of the statue, a person should not drink from this water by placing his mouth to the statue's mouth as it would appear as if he is kissing it.[22]

16. One is forbidden to commission a craftsman to make an idol for himself even if he does not intend to serve it. Also it is forbidden to make an idol with one's own hands even if the idol is meant for someone else and one does not intend to serve it. All the more so, it is forbidden to make an idol with one's own

hands for oneself.[23] (Note: We are given permission to use force, if necessary, to prevent such activities.)

17. It is forbidden to make figures or images for ornamental purposes, even though they are not not idols; that is, one should not make images of gold or silver that are merely for artistic purposes because he might cause others to mistake them for idols. This prohibition pertains to forms with human characteristics in three-dimensional relief. Though forbidden, such actions do not warrant capital punishment.[24]

18. An image that is concave rather than in relief, or two-dimensional such as paintings or woven tapestry, is permitted.

19. It is forbidden to wear a ring that has a seal on it in the image of a man (a cameo) if the image protrudes in relief, but it may be used as a seal. If the image is concave, it may be worn, but it is forbidden to use it as a seal (because the seal creates an image in relief).[25]

20. It is forbidden to form images of the sun or moon or stars or constellations or of the angels or of the four faces (in one form) of the Chariot that Ezekial saw, as it is forbidden to make images of the ministering angels that serve God. Such figures may not even be made in two-dimensional form.

21. According to other opinions, it is forbidden to make forms of the angels and the Chariot only in three-dimensional form (relief). Drawing them on canvas or weaving these images on cloth or painting them on stone would be permitted since this form of expression is not three dimensionial.[26] However, even this latter lenient opinion forbids the drawing of the sun, moon, or stars (in their complete form) in a two-dimensional drawing because they appear to us two-dimensionally in the sky.[27]

22. Concerning a sculpture of man, some say the face by itself is forbidden. Others say that sculpture becomes forbidden only if the whole face is made with its body. According to this second opinion, making a human body with its face is permitted as long

as one does not make the complete body, but only a portion of it. However, it is proper to follow the stricter first opinion[28] (even if the sculpture is made just for beauty).

23. It is not forbidden to keep or physically hold the image of a man unless it is distinctly the image of one worshiped as a god. Any other human image may be kept or held, so long as the image is slightly distorted or damaged, such as by chipping the nose, to dispel any suspicion of its being an idolatrous form. This act of damaging is called nullifying the idol.[29]

24. It is permitted to make statuary of trees and of wild or domestic animals, even of animals which are symbols in astrology, such as the lion, ram, or bull. One may make the full form of these figures and retain them in his possession. However, one may not make one form of all twelve astrological symbols together.[30]

25. There is a further opinion forbidding all three-dimensional forms, whether they are in relief or concave. This opinion forbids making such forms in order to keep them in one's possession. It is proper to heed this opinion.[31]

26. One should never gaze at three-dimensional images of man. Such acts of gazing are spiritually damaging. But images upon a ring, since they are commonly found without idolatrous connotations, may be gazed upon.[32]

27. The three chief idolatrous images in the world are:
   a. The dragon, which is a derivative of the primordial serpent.[33]
   b. A full figure of a man offering the beholder something from the palm of his hand.[34] (This image is commonly found today in front of certain churches.)[35]
   c. A woman nursing an infant. This is the idolatrous perversion of Eve, the mother of all mankind. It became the symbol of the queen of heaven and is an image that still pervades numerous cultures and religions.[36]

PART THREE

1. There is a difference of opinion whether the Children of Noah transgress the commandment of idolatry by convincing someone else to worship an idol. One opinion states that the Children of Noah do not transgress this commandment by leading others to serve an idol. The other opinion states that one is liable for the death penalty, but only if he leads a Jew away from the worship of the God of Israel and convinces him or her to serve an idol. If, however, one Noahite convinces another Noahite to serve an idol, he is not liable for punishment in a court of law, but since he has denied himself and the other person the opportunity of being close to God, he is punished from Heaven.[37]

2. If a person says, "The idol said to me, 'Worship!'" or he says, "God said to me, 'Worship the idol,'" he is a false prophet. If he influences a majority of a city, he is stoned.[38]

3. A seducer is equally liable whether he uses singular or plural expressions in his seduction. For example, if he says, "I will go and worship the idol," or, "Let us go and worship this idol," he is a seducer.

4. One who convinces others to worship him as an idol and says to them, "Serve me," and they worship him, he is stoned to death. If they accept him as their god but do not serve him, he is not stoned.[39]

5. If a prophet prophesies in the name of an idol — if he says for instance, "This particular idol or this particular star said to me that it is an obligation to do such-and-such or not to do such-and-such," — even if his words teach the law correctly, he is subject to the death penalty for idolatry.[40]

6. It is forbidden to establish a law or to refute a law by the authority of someone who prophesies in the name of an idol, nor do we ask him to produce a sign or a miracle. If he does so on his own, we pay no attention to it nor do we reflect about

it. Anyone who thinks about these miracles and says, "Perhaps they are true," transgresses a law.[41] Even if he were to walk on the water or raise the dead, we are to pay no attention to these acts. Such miracles are a test of our faith in God.

7. Similarly, a false prophet is killed by strangulation even if he prophesies in the name of God and teaches the Seven Universal Laws correctly, neither adding nor subtracting from their true meaning.

8. One who prophesies words that he did not hear in a prophetic vision or one who hears the words of a true prophet and says that they were received by him and he prophesies concerning these words, is a false prophet.[42]

9. One who holds himself back from killing a false prophet is a transgressor. And it matters not whether he fears to act because of the false prophet's exalted position, or because he is fearful of the false prophet's words.[43]

(All false prophets, their disciples, and other idolatrous practitioners instill fear in the hearts of their victims, usually by threats of eternal damnation, hellfire, or other similar terrors. One can strengthen his heart against these threats by remembering that God is All-Merciful and rewards and punishes according to a person's deeds, and that even His punishments come as correction and purification of the soul. As King David wrote, "Do not place your trust in benefactors, nor in the son of man in whom there is no salvation. Fortunate is he whose helper is the God of Jacob, whose hope rests upon the Lord his God" (Ps. 146:3,5).

10. A man should not use an idol or a house of idolatry as a signpost, such as telling his friend, "Meet me at the side of this particular house of idolatry."[44]

PART FOUR

1. A pillar that serves as a central point of worship for gatherings of people is called a *matzeva*, a forbidden pillar. It is forbidden even if the people come to it in order to worship God, for this was the way of the ancient idolators. (The Kaaba stone in Mecca is just such a forbidden pillar. And the concept of the forbidden pillar is still with us today in full fashion. The book and film, *2001: A Space Odyssey* were written in praise of the powers of the idolatrous pillar.) Anyone who erects such a pillar performs a forbidden act, but is not killed for it.[45]

2. A stone floor with figures carved on it to attract the eye is called a figured stone and is forbidden. Even if one bows down on it with the intention of honoring God, he performs a forbidden act, for this was the way of the idolator, but he is not killed for it. The way of idol worship was to lay a stone floor such as this before the idol. All stood on the figured stone floor, then bowed before the idol. Therefore, one should not employ a similar practice concerning the worship of God.

3. The previous law applies in all places but the Holy Temple in Jerusalem, where it is permissible to bow down to God upon a stone floor.[46]

4. One who bows down on a figured stone floor does not transgress unless he bows in total prostration, spreading his arms and legs. But if he bows to an actual idol (if the figured stone was only a floor placed before an idol), whether he bows down in complete prostration or merely bows from the waist, he transgresses the prohibition against idolatry and is killed for it.[47]

5. It is commanded to destroy all idols and all things used in serving them and everything that is made because of them, and in the Land of Israel it is commanded to pursue the idol until it is destroyed and driven completely from the land.[48]

6. It is forbidden to derive pleasure or benefit from actual idols

and all items needed for their service or sacrifices (wine, meat, or incense) and all that may be made to beautify them (candles or cloths that are spread out for their honor). Anyone who benefits from any of these transgresses but is not killed for it.[49]

7. One is forbidden any benefit or usage from an animal that has been offered to an idol, including the animal's excrement, its bones, its horns, hooves or skin. Therefore, if there is a skin with a mark on it that indicates this skin was offered to an idol, such as a round hole torn opposite the heart of the animal, this skin is forbidden for use in any way.[50]

8. The difference between an idol belonging to a Noahite and the idol of an Israelite is that the former is forbidden immediately after its making is completed even though it has not yet been served. A Noahite's idol becomes a god from the moment it exists as a graven image. The idol of an Israelite is not forbidden until it is served.[51]

9. A Noahite who inherits an idol from his idolatrous father should cast it into the sea.[52]

10. Figures and images that are made for artistic purposes and not idolatry are permitted for pleasure or profit. Those that appear to have been made for idolatry are forbidden. A statue that holds a staff or a bird or a globe or a sword or a crown and a ring in its hand is presumed to be an idol and it is forbidden for any use (these are all symbols of rulership — the staff because he rules over the world, a bird because it flies above all and its eyes gaze down upon all, a ball because it represents the globe of the earth which he holds in his hand, etc.). Otherwise, it is presumed to be of artistic beauty only and is permitted.[53]

11. Crosses that are publicly displayed are in the category of idols since people give honor to them, remove their hats before them, and bow down or genuflect to them. However, the cross that hangs around a person's neck is considered a memorial and is permitted. Other personal uses like dangling the cross from

the rear view mirror of an automobile are also permitted.[54]

12. However, priests who have crosses in their vestments or around the neck represent something very different from the cross of a person who wears it as a memorial, since the priest stands as a figure of religious authority. Therefore, one must never bow to such priests nor remove the hat in front of them nor do anything that may give the appearance that one worships the cross worn by a priest. If one bows or removes a hat as a gesture of giving honor to God, it must be discreetly away from the presence of such a cross, and preferably prior to the priest's appearance. If it is in a place and a sect where it is known that these worshipers do not bow down to their images, but rather to the honor of the priests that wear them, then one can be lenient to avoid offending these priests. But where it is known that the people bow down to their statues and crosses in a manner that would clearly appear idolatrous, one must be strict and avoid this.

13. One need not be strict about the wearing of a medal around the neck for luck when traveling or the like, since the image on the medal is not worshiped.

14. If one finds vessels such as jewelry or expensive fabrics with images on them, if it is known that these images were made in the name of idol worship such as those found in India and Southeast Asia, they are certainly forbidden. But if one is not sure what the images were made for, or if they are found on nonprecious vessels, such as crude vessels used for water or other foods, they are not forbidden.[55]

15. Today, people are not so attached to their idols, even to the images that they serve, such as the cross or a nursing mother with her child. Because of this, if a vessel is found in Western lands, it can be assumed that the images are for beauty or a memorial and not for idolatry. Thus the vessel would be permitted for use, but it is better not to keep it in one's possession as it might convey the impression that the owner is

an idolator.

16. It is idolatry to consume a food or a drink with the idea that it is the substance of a god and that the person consuming them is therefore assimilating the substance of the god into his own being. (Note: The Children of Noah have historically fallen into idolatrous practices because of a lack of discernment between *Elokah* and *Elokut*, God and Godliness. One can say that all of creation is Godly because it all contains God's life force, but to say that anything of creation is God is idolatry.)

17. It is forbidden to use vessels one finds, upon which appear the figure of a sun or a moon or a dragon, if the vessel is of gold or silver. Similarly if one finds a cloth of silk with scarlet color or rings or earrings with these figures on them, they are forbidden.[56]

18. If one finds these images on other less precious articles, they are permissible because they are presumed to have been made for artistic purposes and to be merely ornamental.

19. Idols and other articles used for their service cause other objects that they become mixed up with to be forbidden, even if the idolatrous articles are but a small factor in the number of objects. For example: if an idol is mixed in with ornamental figures, even if the idol is but one in a thousand of the figures, everything is forbidden and must be thrown into the Dead Sea or similar water where the metal will corrode or be lost.[57]

20. If a person finds money or vessels on the head of an idol, if the items appear to be placed there as an expression of contempt, they are permissible for use. For example: a purse found hanging on the neck of the idol, a cloth draped over its head, a vessel turned upside down and placed on top of its head — all these are permissible. These items were obviously placed there to disgrace the idol, and so it is with anything similar to this.[58] (Of course, if these objects appear to be there to honor the idol, they are forbidden.)

21. If there is a garden or pool with an ornamental idol in it,

one may use either so long as it is not expressly for the benefit
of the idol's priests. But if it is for the priests, it is forbidden
for use.[59]

22. If the garden or pool are there for the idol and for the
general populace, even if the priests use it as well, one may use
it so long as no fee is paid.

23. It is forbidden to trade in a store from which profits are
used for the upkeep of an idol. However, if the profits are
collected by the government and they in turn support the upkeep
of the idol, then it is permissible to trade in the store.[60]

24. If those engaged in the upkeep of idols collect taxes for the
needs of the idols, it is forbidden to pay them any taxes.
However, if the profits first go to the government, which in turn
dispenses money for the upkeep of idols, it is permissible to pay
them taxes.

25. Bread that is given to idolatrous priests is permissible
because this bread is not offered to the idol but is the priests'
portion.[61]

26. Wax candles that were lit before an idol for ornamentation
are forbidden even after they were extinguished because the
intention may have been to relight them. But if they were
extinguished without the intention of relighting, they may be
used. However, even if the candles were knowingly extinguished
without the intention of relighting them, they may not be used
in any way for the honor of God or to fulfill a commandment,
such as to illuminate a house of worship or to have light to study
the Seven Laws of Noah.[62]

PART FIVE

1. Anything that cannot be handled by man or made by man,
even though it is worshiped, is permissible for use. Therefore,
even if idolators worship mountains or hills, trees that grow

naturally or were planted for fruit (excluding those planted originally for idolatrous reasons), public streams (a private stream may have been dug for idolatrous reasons and may therefore be forbidden), or animals, all are permissible for use. And it is permissible to eat fruit that was worshiped so long as it remains in a state of natural growth, attached to the tree or bush, and it is permissible to eat worshiped animals. An animal that is designated for use in idolatry as an offering, prior to its being offered, may be used or eaten. But once the animal is used for the idol, even in the slightest way, it becomes forbidden. For example, if the animal has been slaughtered for idolatry or has been exchanged for an idol or has been exchanged for something that has been exchanged for an idol, it is forbidden, as it is now monetarily equivalent to an idol.[63]

2.   In the above situation, it is assumed that a person's own animal is used for idolatry; but when a person takes another's animal without permission and slaughters it for idolatry or exchanges it, it remains permissible for use. A person cannot cause anything to become forbidden which is not his own.

3.   If one bows down to the earth in its natural state, the ground to which he bows does not become forbidden, but if he digs pits, ditches, or caves in the name of idolatry, this ground becomes forbidden.

4.   If a person bows down to water which has been displaced from its natural state by a wave washing it into a ditch or the like, it is not forbidden water. But if he takes the water in his hand and bows down to it, it becomes forbidden.[64]

5.   Rocks of a mountain that a person worships are permissible so long as they remain in their natural place, but if they are handled and moved, then worshiped, they become forbidden.

6.   If a person erected a pillar or even set up a brick with the intention of worshiping it, but he did not worship it, then other idolators came along and worshiped it, it is forbidden, as this is considered an idolatrous pillar.[65]

7.   A tree planted in order that it may be worshiped as an idol is forbidden. Equally forbidden are its branches, fruit, shade and anything that might give one some kind of benefit. This tree is called an *asherah*, and is specifically mentioned in the Torah (Deut. 16:21).

8.   If a tree is bowed to, although its trunk is permissible, all the shoots and fruit and branches and leaves that come forth during the time that it is worshiped are forbidden.

9.   If idolators watched the fruit of a tree and said that the fruit is there for them to make a drink for an idolatrous temple, and they made the drink and drank it on the day of their festival, this tree is forbidden. It is considered that they planted it for idolatry in the first place and this is why its fruit was used.

10.   If an idol stands underneath a tree, so long as it is there, the tree is forbidden. It is. considered an accessory to idol worship and any pleasure from this tree, even its shade, is forbidden. If the idol is removed, the tree becomes permissible, for the tree itself was never served as an idol.[66]

11.   If a house was not made or served as an idol, but was renovated, plastered, and decorated with images that were inlaid or carved in relief in the name of an idol, one should remove the renovations. They are forbidden because they were made to serve an idol. Then the rest of the house is permissible for use.

12.   If one brings idols into a house, for as long as they are there the house is forbidden for use, as it is considered an accessory to idol worship. Once the idols are removed in a way that indicates a nullification of the house's use as an accessory to them, the house becomes permissible. If the idols were brought there by an idolatrous Noahite, and an Israelite removes them from the house, this does not represent a nullification, because it may be construed that the Noahite wishes the idols to remain, but the Israelite did not. Therefore, just as a Noahite brought the idols into the house, a Noahite must take the idols out of the house in order for it to be considered a nullification of the

house's status as an accessory to idol worship.[67]

13. One may not use a forbidden house in any way. One may not enter it or sit in its shade. However, it is permissible to pass through its shadows.[68]

14. It is also advised that one should distance oneself at least eight feet from the entrance of a house of idol worship.

15. It is forbidden to listen to the music, smell the fragrance, or gaze at the ornaments of idolatrous worship. All the more so, one is forbidden to gaze at the idol itself.

16. If one must walk near a place of idol worship, he should cover his eyes, stop up his ears, and hold his nose to avoid having any sensory benefit from the idolatry. Even if the person has no intention of taking pleasure from these sights, sounds, and smells, he is still bound to conduct himself in the manner described, since he will certainly receive some pleasure from them if he does not so act. And one is obligated to be cautious even in a situation where there are no alternative routes.

17. If an idol rests on a stone, the stone is forbidden for use for as long as the idol is there. When it is removed, the stone is permissible for use.[69]

18. If one has a house with a common wall to a house of idol worship and his house falls, he should not rebuild it as it was, but build it completely within his own property so that he shares no wall with the idolatrous house. The space that remains between his house and the house of idolatry he should fill with thorns or fertilizer in order that the house of idolatry not be enlarged to encroach on his territory. If he has a common wall to an idolatrous house, he should measure the thickness of the wall and the closer half of the wall is his and the other half of the wall belongs to the idolatrous house. The stone or wood or dirt from that other half is forbidden for any use.

19. The proper manner of destroying an idol and all the articles that are forbidden because of it is to grind them to powder and scatter them to the wind, or they should be burned and dumped

into the Dead Sea or a similar body of water to corrode or be forever lost.[70]

20. An idolatrous figure is nullified by chopping off the tip of the nose or the tip of the ear or the tip of the finger or by hammering in a portion of its face (even though no material is lost) or by selling the figure to a Jew who smelts metal. All these constitute nullification.[71] Once nullified, the figure is permissible to own and use.[72]

21. An idol or any accessory to an idol, if it is nullified as an idol, becomes permissible for use. But anything that is offered up to the idol remains forbidden forever, and nullification is of no help.[73] (Nullification must be performed by the one who worshiped the idol. If one who did not worship the idol nullifies it, the act accomplishes nothing.)[74]

22. An idol worshiped by Jews can never be nullified, even if a Noahite owned it in partnership with a Jew. It is forbidden forever and must be destroyed. Similarly, if the idol of a Noahite comes into the hand of a Jew and afterward the Noahite nullifies it, his nullification is of no help at all. It is forbidden forever.

23. An Israelite cannot nullify the idol of a Noahite, even if it is in the domain of the Noahite and the latter gave the Jew permission to nullify it. Only a Noahite can nullify his own idol.

24. A minor or a fool cannot nullify an idol.

25. The nullification of an idol automatically nullifies its accessories. But if only the accessories were nullified, although they are permissible for use, the idol itself remains forbidden.

26. Vessels that an idolatrous priest holds in his hand, such as a goblet, an incense tray, or a recorder or other musical instrument, are considered accessories and require nullification.[75]

27. If the idolatrous figure is given as collateral or sold to a Noahite or to an Israelite who does not smelt it, or if it falls onto a garbage pile and is not cleaned away, or it was stolen by

robbers and the articles were not reclaimed, or if one spat in front of it or urinated in front of it or one dragged it on the ground or threw it into excrement, it is still forbidden as these do not constitute nullification.[76]

28. If the worshipers abandoned an idol and it is a time of peace, it is permissible for use (as a nutcracker, etc.) because it is considered nullified (since they did not take it with them, it shows that they no longer value it). But if it is a time of war, it is forbidden because it is assumed they abandoned it only because of the war.[77]

29. If an idol broke in half by itself or by accident, the broken pieces are forbidden until they are nullified. Therefore, if one finds broken pieces of an idol, they are forbidden for use because it is possible its worshipers did not nullify it.

30. If the idol was made in pieces that fit together so that the average person could reassemble it, one has to nullify each separate piece. If the idol cannot be reassembled, only one limb need be nullified.

31. An idol's altar that becomes damaged is still forbidden for use or for any gain or benefit until the major portion of it has been smashed by the idolaters.[78]

PART SIX

1. One who consorts with ghosts or raises spirits to know hidden things or to know the future, and who does it of his own free will and intentionally, is liable for idolatry.[79] (A Noahite is permanently warned about these things, so that he can never claim that he did not know the law.)

2. If a person stands and burns incense and waves a myrtle branch in his hand and speaks whispered words to summon a being, then hears the summoned being speak to him, and if the being answers what it is asked in words that are below the earth

in a very deep voice that is not recognized by the ear but felt in the thoughts; and if the practitioner takes the skull of a dead person and offers incense to it and uses arts of divination with whispers and various other rituals to the skull until he hears a low voice proceeding forth from under his armpit — all these acts come under the category of raising ghosts, and the practitioner is killed for doing them.

3. If a person places the bone of a certain bird or other kind of creature in his mouth and offers incense and performs other rituals until he falls to the ground like one stricken with an epileptic seizure, and if he speaks while in this trance things that will happen in the future, this is a form of idolatry and he is killed for it.[80]

4. It is a matter of dispute whether a Noahite is forbidden to perform acts of witchcraft.[81] If the final law is according to those who forbid it,[82] the wizard or witch is found guilty and given the penalty of death by stoning.

(Note: Inasmuch as such practices attach the practitioner to evil spiritual forces, they are harmful to his soul. As for those who proclaim that there is no such thing today as real witchcraft — and they are the same ones who say there is no such thing today as real idolatry — these people are ignorant and naive. Witchcraft as well as idol worship exist in the most complete meaning of the terms. Voodoo rites and satanic covens are flourishing today in England, the United States, Japan and throughout the rest of the world just as they did in ancient Egypt. We can even bear witness to a popular force in contemporary music; certain rock-and-roll groups that have declared themselves agents and disciples of Satan. Teenagers and adults by the tens of millions have naively become enamored with these groups and their philosophies, which advocate sexual perversion and often physical cruelty. In effect, the fans of these rock groups are disciples of disciples of the satanic forces. Even though the dark side powers "cannot do evil, neither is it in them to do good" (Jer. 10:5), nevertheless one is well advised to avoid them, lest he give them power by acknowledging them. The protection against these negative rites and their results is to remember that evil as well as good come solely from God, the Master of all forces, and He brings evil forth in order to bestow free will to man so he can earn either reward or punishment.)

5.   There is also a dispute concerning the permissibility of divination, the act of interpreting signs. Some authorities hold that it is forbidden and idolatrous, while others contend that it is permissible and even meritorious, approaching the level of prophecy, and that great and holy sages engaged in such practices.[83]

6.   How does one engage in divination? For example, one might say, "Since my bread fell from my mouth or my staff fell from my hand, I will not go to a certain place today, because if I go today, my needs will not be done," or, "Since a fox passed on my right side, I will not go out of my house today, for if I do, a sneaky individual will meet me and trick me."[84]

7.   Similarly, those who hear a bird calling and say, "It will be thus and it will not be thus," or, "It will be good to do thus and it will not be good to do thus," are engaging in divination.

8.   Also, if a person proposes conditions, saying, "If such-and-such happens to me, I will do such-and-such, but if it does not happen to me, I will not do it," he is performing an act of divination.

9.   Everything that is similar to the foregoing is divination. But even according to the opinion that considers it forbidden, divination is not punishable by the courts.

10.   Certain interpretations of signs are considered permissible by all, however. It is not wrong to say, "This house that I built has been a good-luck sign from the moment I built it," or, "My wife has been a blessing, for from the moment I married her, I started becoming wealthy," or, "This animal that I acquired has brought me luck, for from the moment I got it, I started

becoming wealthy."[85]

11. And similarly, if someone asks a child, "What verse did you learn?" if the child tells him something that indicates a blessing, and the person becomes happy and says, "This is a good sign," he does no wrong.

12. The difference of opinion occurs only when a person determines future actions by the interpretations of signs. A person who merely acknowledges a sign for something that already occurred is not practicing divination. There is another opinion that permits the interpreting of a sign to determine future action if the specific sign has proven successful three times in the past.

13. What is magic? It is engaging in exercises or disciplines that bring one to a euphoric state or that interrupt normal thought processes in order to proclaim future events. One might say, "Thus-and-so will happen in the future or it will not happen," or he might say, "It is advisable to be careful of thus-and-so."[86]

14. There are those who engage in magic who use a stone or sand, and there are those who bend down toward the earth and move around and emit screams. There are those who look into a brass mirror or a crystal ball, then predict the future to one who is seeking this knowledge. There are those who lift a staff in their hands and lean on it and strike it until they augment their thought processes so as to be able to speak about the future.

(Note: Many cities abound today with practitioners of these rites, which include palmistry, tarot cards, phrenology, and many other similar practices. Many practitioners have established businesses and advertise their services freely. To avail oneself of such practices is an act of faith in powers other than God's. What little gain might come from going to such practitioners will certainly be more than offset by one's separation from God because of involvement with these negative influences.)

15. Moreover, one who uses illusion to captivate the spectators by showing them things that are not in the natural order of things, and who makes it appear to the spectators that the illusionist did a miraculous deed, he is in this category, and such actions are forbidden as they lead to idolatrous practices.[87]

16. It is forbidden to practice magic or to consult one who practices magic, but the courts do not punish for the practice of magic or for consulting a practitioner of magic.[88] (One must be reminded that in all instances of transgression that are outside the jurisdiction of the courts, the transgressor is punished by the hand of Heaven.)

17. It is forbidden to be an astrological observer of the times. What is an observer of times? It is one who gives certain times that, according to astrology, indicate that such a day is good and such a day is bad, such a day is proper to do thus-and-so and on such a day one should not do thus-and-so, or such a year or such a month is bad for such a thing.[89]

18. Astrological forecasts are in a different category from using astrology to understand a person's characteristics and natural tendencies, the latter being a permissible practice.

19. Observing of times is forbidden even if the observer of times does not perform any action but merely conveys falsehoods to gullible people and convinces them that these are words of truth and contain wisdom. All who conduct themselves and their activities because of astrological forecasts, working at a certain time or traveling at a certain time determined by the astrologers, transgress the law, but the courts do not punish them for this.[90]

20. What is a charmer? This is one who speaks words that are not of the language of people and have no essence nor understanding. None of the vulgar sounds or words or spoken names of the charmer contain the power to cause harm, nor do they do any good at all. But gullible people accept such things to the point where they will believe a charmer when he says, "If you will say such-and-such to a poisonous snake, it can do you

no harm," or, "If a person has such-and-such said to him, he is protected from harm."[91]

21. The charmer might hold a key or a stone or any object while he says his nonsensical things. Anything similar to this is in the category of dealing in charms, and both the charmer and the one subjecting himself to the charmer transgress the law, but neither are punished by the courts.

22. If a person was bitten by a poisonous snake or stung by a scorpion, he is permitted to whisper any kind of spell he chooses over the place of the wound if he thinks it will help. This is just so the person, who is in mortal danger, can put his mind at ease and take courage. And even though what he says will certainly not help at all, since he is in danger, he is allowed to do it to avoid panicking.[92]

23. One who whispers spells over another's wound or reads verses from the Torah over someone who is sick or dying, or similarly one who reads verses over a child to prevent the child from becoming fearful, is worse than one who is in the category of a diviner or a charmer, because by using the Holy Scriptures like this to cure the body, he denies the truth of the Torah, which comes as a cure for the soul. But if one studies appropriate parts of the Torah or reads Psalms in order that the merit of reading them should protect him and save him from danger and harm, this is permissible.[93] (Of course, it is best to pray to God for protection and healing of every kind.)

24. What is a necromancer? This is one who starves himself and sleeps overnight in a cemetery in order to bring the dead to him in a dream to inform him of something.[94]

25. There are also those who wear certain clothing and speak incantations and offer incense and sleep alone in order to bring a specific dead person to come and speak to them in a dream.

26. In general, all who do various rites in order to summon the dead so as to learn information are in the category of necromancers and they transgress the law, but they are not

punished by the courts for it.

27. It is forbidden to consult one who raises ghosts or spirits, because these practitioners are liable to the death penalty. One who consults with these practitioners but does not do the rituals transgresses, but he is not punished by the courts.[95]

28. One who does not practice real witchcraft but merely uses sleight of hand or other illusions to fool onlookers transgresses the law but is not punished by the courts for it. It is, however, a serious matter, as such illusions are found in true witchcraft.[96] (But witchcraft is definitely not an illusion. If it were, why would one performing it be subject to the death penalty? Witchcraft is a receptacle for the impure husks that surround holiness and divert it from its true purpose.)

29. All the foregoing are acts of deception and are false things, and through them the idolator deceives the people of the world in order to gain a following. (Note: Without a single exception, the numerous cults, pseudoreligions, false messiahs, and demigods that are prevalent in the world today employ idolatrous practices to achieve spiritual power. Like the false prophets, they all use spritual threats concomitant with their promises of salvation. Those who take refuge in these deceivers and find goodness in them, be warned: evil seldom announces itself as evil, otherwise all but a very few would avoid it. Evil almost always announces itself as good and beneficial and always mixes truth and goodness with its destructive lies. Herein lies its power.) But all who are wise and possess true knowledge know by clear proofs that all these idolatrous practices are empty and vain and contain no value at all. Those who are drawn to such things lack understanding and depart from the way of truth.[97] Because of this, the Torah instructs everyone concerning these foolish vanities, "Be wholehearted with the Lord your God" (Deut. 18:13), meaning that people should put their trust in God and know that everything that comes to them comes from Him.[98]

Chapter Six
Blasphemy

PART ONE

1. Blasphemy is the act of cursing the Creator. It is a deed so indescribably heinous that the Talmud, whenever referring to blasphemy, calls it by the euphemistic term "blessing God," to avoid directly expressing the idea of cursing God, the Father of all.

2. Blasphemy is the only means by which one transgresses the Seven Universal Commandments through the faculty of speech alone.

3. Blasphemy falls into the category of revenge. When someone is harmed by a person and seeks revenge, he may shout at the person or curse him. If the harm is great, the one seeking vengeance may not be satisfied by words alone but may physically strike out at the one who harmed him. In extreme cases, the vengeful person may not be satisfied till he kills. This is between a man and his neighbor. Between man and God it is somewhat different. Man cannot kill God nor can he strike Him physically. The ultimate revenge that man can take against God is to curse Him. Therefore, blasphemy is seen as the expression of the desire to hurt God, even to erase His existence or murder Him.

4. The prohibition against blasphemy comes to teach us not to speak evil against God nor to detract from His exaltedness in any way by intentionally using words to lessen the reverence

and faith that are due Him.[1]

5. As with any of the Seven Universal Commandments, before one can be tried in a court of law for having transgressed a commandment, there must be a witness to the deed who is willing to testify against the accused. This poses a problem, for how can the witness testify against the accused unless he repeats the blasphemous expression used, which would be a further transgression of this commandment?

6. In the Jewish courts of law, the matter was handled in the following manner. The witnesses during the entirety of the trial were directed to use a euphemistic phrase for the actual blasphemous utterance that they heard, eliminating reference to God in the phrase.[2] Then, at the conclusion of the proceedings, the courtroom was cleared of all but those essential to the trial, and the witnesses were obliged to repeat the actual blasphemy that they heard. Upon hearing the blasphemy, the judges rent their garments as one does for the death of a parent or any other tragedy that elicits grief.

7. Rabbi Chiya declared that after the destruction of the Second Temple, one who heard blasphemy was no longer required to rend his garments, otherwise all would be walking around with their garments in tatters.[3]

8. The Code of Jewish Law, which is the final word in determining the religious obligations of the Jew, states that a person who hears blasphemy is commanded to place the blasphemer under a ban of excommunication, regardless of whether the blasphemy was uttered against God's Name or any of His divine attributes, whether in the Hebrew language or any of the other languages of the world, or whether the blasphemer was a Jew or a Gentile.[4] This ban of excommunication means that the person has no rights as a member of the community and that all are forbidden to speak to him.

9. Profaning the Lord of Hosts with one's lips, God forbid, is a transgression similar to, but worse than, idolatry. Whereas

idolatry is the act of worshiping a creation and thereby denying the true existence of the Creator, blasphemy is an acknowledgment of His existence but a denial of His greatness or His goodness. The blasphemer denies the truth that everything comes directly from God solely for mankind's benefit and as a bestowal of goodness. Often the goodness is unrevealed, as with a person's pain and suffering. At these times, one with a coarse consciousness or without a sufficient degree of faith in God can come to verbally express dissatisfaction with his lot through blasphemy, and thus transgress the law.[5]

10. We see the essence of this problem in the Book of Job. Job, God's faithful servant, was struck by Satan with boils from the soles of his feet to the crown of his head. As he sat in agony from the affliction, his wife scolded him, saying, "Are you still holding fast to your integrity? Curse God, and die." But he answered her, "You speak as one who is despicable. Should we accept only the good from God and not also accept the evil? With all this, Job did not sin with his lips" (Job 2:9-10).

11. Consistent with this, it is a Jewish tradition to bless God for the bad as well as for the good.[6] Even when, God forbid, one hears news of a person's death, he responds by saying, *Baruch Dayan Emet* (Blessed be the True Judge).[7]

12. Blasphemy as an expression of an incomplete faith in God is epitomized by the false notion that there are two powers and two kingdoms, God's and Satan's. All such theology denies that God is the Lord and Master of all.

13. The Book of Job shows clearly that God is the Ruler of Satan as well as of everyone and everything else, for when Satan wishes to test Job, he first petitions God for permission, whereby God sets definite boundaries for Satan, commanding him not to take Job's life, saying, "Behold, he is in thy hand, but guard his life" (Job 2:6).

14. The teaching in Christian theology that the evil force rebelled against the Lord and set up a separate kingdom is

76

tantamount to blasphemy, for it denigrates the Creator and denies His infinite majesty.

15. Some authorities state that false oaths or meaningless oaths whereby one invokes the Name of God are forbidden under the category of blasphemy.[8] An example of a false oath would be for one to take an oath in God's Name that a tree is a rock, and a meaningless oath would be for one to swear in God's Name that a tree is a tree. There is a difference of opinion as to whether one who delays fulfilling an oath violates the law.[9]

PART TWO

1. The prohibition of blasphemy is transgressed even if one uses another term for God, for example, an attribute or epithet such as the Merciful One, the Father, or any other descriptive term. No matter how one curses God, and no matter in what language, the one who transgresses this commandment is subject to the death penalty by a court of law.[10]

2. If anyone acknowledges that an idolatry is true, even though he does not serve it, it is as if he reviles and blasphemes the mighty and exalted Name of God. Whether a person is an idolator or a blasphemer, it is the same in that both deny God.[11]

3. One who blasphemes and instantly retracts his words is nonetheless guilty if he blasphemed in front of witnesses. If he blasphemes in private and his words are heard by no one other than himself and his Creator, let him repent and God will forgive his transgression.[12]

4. One who curses God in the name of idolatry is subject to being attacked and killed by zealots, who are, in turn, held harmless by the law. But one who is not a zealot, but seeks reprisal against a transgressor because of a desire for justice, must begin proceedings through due process of law against the accused.

(Note: A zealot is one who serves God with a selfless, passionate love and is jealous for God's honor. Reacting to a desecration of God's Name, the zealot takes immediate action to stop the desecration. If one has to ponder the situation or ask the opinion of another, wiser than he in such matters, his hesitation or intellectual inquiry takes him out of the category of the zealot, and he is forbidden to take action. The scriptural source for the action of a zealot is seen in the heroics of Phineas, who stopped a plague among the Children of Israel when he slew a prince of the tribe of Simeon and the Midianite woman with whom he was having forbidden sexual relations (Num. 25:7-8).

5. It should be the goal of every one of the Children of Noah to strive to do more than the minimum that the law requires, for this is the idea of piety, and one who accepts the responsibility of fulfilling the Seven Laws of Noah is called one of the pious of the nations. Bearing this in mind, a person is well advised to withhold speaking evil about his fellow man as well as against his Creator, for in God's image was man created, and one who reviles his fellow insults God as well. If, by words alone, one destroys a favorable picture of a person in another's mind, this is considered killing him. And it matters not whether the destructive words are true or false.

6. Striving to go beyond the letter of the law has no limit, for the commandments of God are as deep as the ocean and as wide as the sky.[13] Since everything in creation reflects the hand of the Creator, a truly pious person withholds himself from speaking negatively against anything. There are times, however, when it is appropriate and even mandatory to speak out against someone. For instance, when someone is engaged in wicked pursuits and it appears that others will follow his lead, then it becomes a great kindness and even an obligation to speak in condemnation of the transgressor.[14] But in the main, gossip, calumny, and tale-bearing, even when the statements are true,

will stand in the way of the individual's spiritual and moral growth.[15]

Chapter Seven
Murder

1. The commandment prohibiting murder is explicitly stated to Noah by God: "Whoever sheds the blood of man, by man shall his blood be shed, for He made man in the image of God" (Gen. 9:6).

2. A Noahite who kills a human being, even a baby in the womb of its mother, receives the death penalty. This means that one who strikes a pregnant woman, thereby killing the fetus, incurs the death penalty.[1] (The act must have been done at least forty days after conception.[2] Before forty days, the act is in the category of destruction of man's seed, and the transgressor is liable for punishment from heaven, not by a court on earth.)

3. Men and women have an equal responsibility to observe the prohibition against murder, and any act for which a man is held liable, a woman is equally held liable.[3]

4. If a person kills one who is terminally ill or is falling from the top of a cliff or is certain to die momentarily for any other reason, he transgresses the prohibition against murder and is liable for punishment by the courts.[4] This judgment places the idea of mercy killing or euthanasia squarely in the category of murder.

5. If one pushes a person onto railway tracks and a train subsequently comes and kills him, or if one leaves a person in a situation where he will surely starve to death, although the action only indirectly causes the person's death, it is murder and the act is punishable by the courts.

6. If a person sees someone pursuing another for the obvious or suspected intent of committing murder or with the intent of causing the pursued to commit a sin, and the observer is able to stop the pursuer by wounding him, but kills him instead, he transgresses this commandment and receives the death penalty. If, however, the person himself is being pursued, he is free to take any action necessary to save his own life.[5]

7. Authorities disagree as to whether it is permissible for a Noahite to kill a fetus in order to save the life of the mother. But all agree that taking the mother's life to save the fetus is murder and punishable by the courts.[6]

8. If a Noahite kills someone through a messenger, both the messenger and the one who sent him are liable for punishment as murderers.[7]

9. A person is commanded to allow himself to be killed rather than kill. This means that if people try to compel a person on pain of death to kill someone, he must not commit murder regardless of the consequences.[8]

10. Suicide is forbidden under the Seven Universal Laws.[9]

11. There is no place of legal refuge for a murderer. Any relative (on the father's side) of a murder victim who can legally inherit property of the deceased may designate himself a "blood avenger." If the murder was committed intentionally with malice aforethought, it is the blood avenger's obligation to see that the murderer is brought to trial.

12. If the killing was manslaughter — that is, if the killer acted unintentionally but negligently, and it is a matter of a *ger toshav* (proselyte at the gate, a Noahite who lives according to the Seven Universal Commandments) killing another *ger toshav,* the killer flees to a designated city of refuge until his trial comes up. If the courts rule that he did kill but unintentionally, he must return to the city of refuge and reside there until the High Priest of the Jews dies (the death of the righteous is an atonement for the generation), then he is free to return to his home. If he leaves

the city of refuge prior to the death of the High Priest, the blood avenger may find him and kill him. The blood avenger is held harmless for killing the manslaughterer.

If a *ger toshav* kills an Israelite unintentionally but negligently, or if he kills another *ger toshav* because he thought that it was permissible (this is considered tantamount to killing intentionally), he is liable for the death penalty.

If a Noahite who does not live according to the Seven Universal Commandments kills another Noahite in a circumstance of manslaughter, he is subject to the death penalty and the city of refuge affords him no protection.

In any case where a blood avenger kills the manslaughterer, if a relative of the slain manslaughterer seeks revenge against the blood avenger and kills him, that relative is deemed a murderer and is prosecuted as such.[10]

13. There is a difference of opinion as to whether the Seven Universal Commandments include the commandment forbidding the willful destruction of a man's seed through masturbation or any other act of wasting semen.[11] All agree, however, that sexual relations with a woman who is incapable of bearing children is not considered wasting semen. One opinion is that the commandment to be fruitful and multiply, having been given to Noah, but not repeated to Moses, was in force only during those generations before the historical event of Mount Sinai. In those early times, wasting semen was considered among the most heinous of sins and a chief reason that God brought the Flood to destroy the world. Moreover, the Torah clearly teaches that Judah's two sons, Er and Onan, were killed by God, for "the thing which he (Onan) did was evil in the eyes of the Lord" (Gen. 38:10). But this event also occurred before the giving of the Torah on Mount Sinai. This opinion concludes that since the commandment against wasting seed was not repeated at Mount Sinai, it is no longer in effect as part of the Seven Universal Commandments.[12]

The other opinion states that despite its not being repeated at Mount Sinai, since it was originally part of the Seven Universal Commandments, a man must not willfully destroy his seed, though the act is not punishable by the courts. After a man has fulfilled his minimal obligation of bringing a son and a daughter into the world, if he wishes then to use contraceptive devices, he should use those types that do not act directly on the semen.[13] Also, according to this viewpoint, masturbation would be strictly forbidden.

In spiritual terms, the reason for the great concern and strictness concerning the wasting of a man's seed is that it is considered the willful destruction of his life-giving force and equated with life itself. Therefore, the destruction of a man's seed is related closely to murder, and more, to the murder of his own children.

Sexual Relations

1.   It is written, "Therefore a man shall leave his father and his mother and shall cling to his wife and they shall be one flesh" (Gen. 2:24). According to the Holy Spirit this verse comes to instruct mankind concerning forbidden relationships.[1] Rashi comments that the phrase, "Therefore a man shall leave his father and his mother," forbids the man to have sexual relations with the wife of his father (not his mother) even after the death of his father, when she is no longer considered a married woman. Obviously, this also includes his natural mother. The phrase, "cling to his wife," comes to teach us that he shall have relations with his own wife and not another man's wife. "To his wife" comes to teach us that he shall have relations with the opposite sex, not with a male. "And they shall be of one flesh" comes to exclude any animal, for an animal is not of one flesh with a man.[2]

2.   A Noahite is forbidden to have relationships with certain relatives and others to whom he or she is not related. These are:
>   Mother (even if his birth had been the result of her having been seduced or raped)
>   Father
>   Daughter
>   Father's sister
>   Mother's sister[3]

3.   Under the Seven Universal Laws, one is permitted to have relations with individuals related through marriage after the

death of the relative. According to some opinions, this even includes a man's father's wife (not his mother) after his father dies. Those falling in this category are:

Father's wife (not one's mother)
Brother's wife
Wife's sister
Daughter-in-law
Stepdaughter.

4. It is the opinion of some authorities that the father's wife is forbidden even after the death of the father, and the prohibition is thought to include women that the father merely had relations with, even if they were seduced or raped by the father.[4] Other authorities permit relations with the father's wife after his death, but forbid relations with either the father's or the mother's maternal sister.

5. It is argued in the name of Rabbi Akiva that all relationships that warrant the death penalty in a Jewish court of law also will receive the death penalty in a Noahite court of law. This includes a relationship that exists through marriage (with a mother-in-law or daughter-in-law). The reason is that since one's father's wife is forbidden, this is extended to include others related through marriage (a mother-in-law being related through marriage). Such relationships are punishable by the courts.[5] Other authorities say that only the father's wife is in this forbidden category, and they exclude other relatives through marriage.[6]

6. Forbidden relationships, other than with relatives, are:
A man with another man's wife
A male with a male
A person (male or female) with an animal[7]

7. A man is forbidden to have relations with another man's wife, whether she is the wife of another Noahite or the Jewish wife of a Jew.[8] Although a Jewish man is forbidden to marry a

85

Noahite woman and from the perspective of the Jewish man there is no marriage, nevertheless, the bond of marriage exists for her and she is forbidden to other men. Under the Seven Universal Commandments, a woman is considered to be a man's wife when the couple has sexual relations with the intent that it constitute marriage.[9]

8. A man is not punished by the courts for having relations with a married woman unless he has sexual intercourse with her in the normal manner (vaginal penetration), inasmuch as this is considered to be the way for a man to be with a woman.[10] But with other forbidden relationships, a man is liable for punishment for sodomy or any other sexual act; it does not have to be the normal way of intercourse.[11]

9. A man is liable for punishment even if there was only slight penetration during the act of intercourse.[12] However, some are of the opinion that one is not liable for only slight penetration.[13]

10. A man is not punished by the courts for having relations with a married woman until she has consummated her marriage with her husband. But if she is engaged and not yet married, even if she is standing under the wedding canopy, and there has been no consummation of the marriage, he is not liable for punishment by the courts. By this law, we are referring to a Noahite man with a Noahite woman. Regarding a Noahite man and an Israelite woman, whether she has consummated the marriage or is engaged and has not yet consummated the marriage or married but has not consummated the marriage, he is liable for capital punishment.[14]

11. In times of slavery, if a Noahite man designated a specific female slave for his male slave and then had relations with her, he was killed because of it. She was considered another man's wife. However, the master was not condemned until it had become public knowledge that those particular slaves had been given to each other. And when did she become permissible again? When she separated from him and uncovered her head

in the marketplace (that is, demonstrated publicly that she was available to any man).[15]

12. The concept of divorce with regard to Noahites is a matter of dispute. One opinion holds that there is no divorce possible.[16] Another opinion states that no writ of divorce is necessary, rather that divorce is dependent solely on the volition of either spouse, even if one of them is against the divorce. They separate due to the desire of either one and the thing is done.[17] Others contend that the woman may divorce her husband, but that the husband may not divorce his wife.[18]

13. One who caresses a forbidden member of the opposite sex, or hugs or kisses in a manner of lust, or has close personal contact for the sake of pleasure, transgresses the commandment prohibiting forbidden relationships, but he is not punished by the courts. In all cases where the courts are not empowered to act, punishment is meted out by God.[19]

14. It is forbidden to signal with the hands or the feet or to wink at any person who is in the category of a forbidden relationship. One should not be frivolous or light-headed with anyone in this category, nor should a man deliberately smell the perfume or gaze at the beauty of a woman who is forbidden.[20]

15. A man is guilty of transgressing the commandment forbidding illicit sexual relations by having relations with a male whether the male is an adult or a child, whether the male is consenting, coerced or forced, in public or in the privacy of one's own domicile.[21]

(Note: In the Holy Scriptures, of all the illicit sexual relationships mentioned, only homosexuality is described as an "abomination to God." Even bestiality is not so described. From a spiritual perspective, homosexuality is devastating, destroying both the body and the soul of those who engage in it. No homosexual was ever born into this world through a homosexual relationship. And although it is true that a person may have congenital tendencies towards homosexuality, it is like

87

the child with the trait of tearing out its hair or banging its head against the wall. If the tendency is destructive, the goal is to seek correction. When a person is ill, the goal is to help him get well.

Ultimately, homosexuals themselves will complain against those who misled them by condoning their practices and encouraging them, including the politicians who pander to them as a constituency. In the end they will see that this deviation brings one to excessive, abnormal weakness and to horrible diseases as we are *beginning* to discover.[22] In the context of history, every society that encouraged or condoned homosexuality was short-lived, terminated even at the height of its glory. Most notable of these, of course, was ancient Greece, which ruled the world and then was summarily voided in its prime. Ironically, it was the tiny Jewish nation led by the priestly Maccabees that broke the back of the mighty Greek Empire. It is no wonder then that Jewish religionists are so outraged at this society's permissive attitude towards homosexuality, which is the essence of Western society's corrupting Hellenistic legacy.)

16. Though it violates the spirit of the Seven Universal Commandments, lesbianism is not explicitly stated as one of the forbidden relationships. Lesbianism is, however, deemed an immoral and unnatural relationship that destroys the order of the world. Prostitution is in the same general category; that is, while not strictly forbidden, it is outside the realm of morality and therefore violates the spirit of the Seven Universal Laws.

17. Relations with an animal are forbidden at any stage of the animal's maturity, even the day of its birth. A Noahite who has sexual relations with an animal is liable for punishment, but the animal is not killed. In the case of a Jew copulating with an animal, both the person and the animal are killed.

18. The Children of Noah are considered related only through the mother. Those on the father's side are not considered

relatives.[23] This means that a man's half-sister (of the same father but a different mother) is not considered related to him and is permissible to him.[24]

19. There is an argument in the Talmud as to whether a Noahite is permitted to have a relationship with his daughter inasmuch as she is not considered his relative.[25] The conclusion is that, despite the fact that his daughter is not considered to be his relative, she is nonetheless forbidden because she is in the same category as his mother (a parent-child relationship), and his mother is forbidden.[26]

20. In a homosexual or bestial act, one is liable even if there is only partial penetration.[27]

21. It is forbidden under the Seven Universal Commandments to castrate any male, whether man or animal or fowl. This aspect of the law correlates to both the Laws of Forbidden Relations and the Laws of the Limb of a Living Animal. In one opinion, castration of oneself is a transgression, but it is questionable whether it is a transgression to fulfill someone's request to castrate him or even to agree to castrate an animal of his,[28] despite its clearly being an act of maiming one of God's creatures.[29] Nevertheless, even with so bizarre and irreversible an act as castration, repentance and forgiveness are possible through God's great mercy, as it is written, "For thus has said the Lord concerning the eunuchs that keep My Sabbaths and choose that which pleases Me, and take hold of My covenant. I will give to them within My house and within My walls a place and a name better than sons and daughters; and an everlasting name will I give them that will not be cut off" (Isa. 56:4-5).

Chapter Nine
Theft

1. Of all the categories of the Seven Universal Commandments, the prohibition against theft may be the hardest to obey. Human history and psychology are in clear agreement with the Talmudic statement, that "Man's soul has a craving and longing for incest and robbery."[1] But committing theft, unlike incest, is often a simple matter in which the opportunity presents itself almost constantly. Moreover, the commandment against theft includes aspects that, without thorough study, might elude a person and be thought of as acceptable behavior. Therefore, a frequent review of the laws of theft is important.

2. Theft in the Seven Universal Commandments is one general category with many parts and is virtually identical to Torah Law, which has sixteen commandments dealing with the subject of taking what does not belong to oneself. This means that God's will concerning theft is virtually identical whether the person involved is an Israelite or a Noahite. The only difference involves the return of a stolen object worth less than a *pruta*[2] (the smallest coin denomination in the times of the Talmud). If such an object is stolen from a Jew, it need not be returned, for the Israelite is willing to forgive the theft of so small an object and forego its return; but the Noahite does not forego an object worth less than a *pruta,* and such a stolen object must therefore be returned to him.[3]

3. The commandment prohibiting theft holds men and women equally liable in every aspect and detail.[4]

4.   One is liable for punishment whether he brazenly robs in public or sneaks into a house on a moonless night.[5]

5.   One is liable whether he steals money or any object or kidnaps a person. And he is liable no matter from whom he steals.

6.   A Noahite who steals a beautiful woman from the enemy during time of war is liable for punishment. It is presumed that he kidnapped her and that she is a married woman.[6]

7.   The Children of Noah are forbidden to engage in wars of land conquest, but if such a war does occur, and in the process a land is conquered, what the Noahite acquires of this new land belongs to him *ex post facto*.

8.   Later authorities rule that a man who rapes or seduces a woman who is not forbidden to him is liable for punishment because he is stealing from the woman's worth for his own personal use.[7] This judgment applies only to a man who seduces a woman, not to a woman who seduces a man. A woman is considered unable to truly seduce or rape a man, as a man must have an erection to have intercourse and therefore his involvement in the act is one of acceptance and volition.

9.   The early Sages were in disagreement as to whether the Children of Noah were warned concerning usury and over-pricing before the giving of the Torah.[8] In either case, these commandments are both in effect today because they were given to Moses at Mount Sinai, not because God commanded Noah to follow them. (A general principle of the Seven Universal Commandments is that they are binding only because they were given on Mount Sinai.) The great sage Nachmanides (Rabbi Moses ben Nachman, also known as Ramban), states that overcharging is clearly one of the tenets of the commandment prohibiting theft.[9] This means that a transaction whereby one is greatly overcharged is considered an illegal transaction and may be voided. Usury, the act of lending money at unfair interest rates, is in the same category and is forbidden and

considered an illegal transaction.

10. In the category of overcharging is the admonition against using false weights and measures. This applies to any storeowner or salesperson, whether he is selling fish or precious stones, or measuring land for sale, as it is written, "You shall do no unrighteousness in judgment, in measuring land, in weight, or in measuring liquids" (Lev. 19:35). And inasmuch as the act of false weighing and measuring is forbidden, it is similarly forbidden to have such false weights or measuring devices in one's possession, as it is written, "You shall not have in your bag diverse weights, a great and a small" (Deut. 25:13).

11. The idea here is that since one's sustenance comes from the hand of God, a man should earn it through honesty, not chicanery. In Talmudic times, the fair amount of profit gained was thought to be one-sixth,[10] but since profit margins are considered somewhat relative and subjective, the fair amount remains to be determined by the norms set in each generation.

12. A Noahite is not obligated to return an object that he stole. But since he stole it, he is held accountable for the prescribed punishment in a court of law. This is according to Rashi's opinion, which holds that when a single act warrants two punishments, the stricter punishment is enforced and the lesser one is foregone. Other authorities argue that this principle applies only to the Jew and the laws of the Torah, and that when a Noahite has stolen, he is obligated to return the stolen article to its rightful owner, despite the fact that he has incurred the death penalty.[11]

13. One may well ask why the thief, who is going to be executed anyway, should bother to return the stolen object. He could just as well leave it to his spouse or child or a friend and therefore have some indirect benefit. The explanation goes right to the heart of the intent of God's Law, which is just and merciful at the same time. Every punishment meted out through the justice of the Noahide courts serves as an atonement, sparing

the transgressor punishment in the Eternal World. This, of course, assumes that the convicted criminal repents for his transgression and returns to God before he is executed. Because of the justice of the courts, therefore, a man can transgress and still receive a share of the World to Come as a righteous person.

14. What happens then, if a man commits a crime and is not punished by the courts? Suppose there are two men, one who killed negligently but without premeditation and another who killed with malice aforethought. There were no witnesses to either crime. God will bring the two men together through Divine Providence. For instance, on a crowded street, the one who killed unintentionally might be driving a car, while the killer is crossing the street as a pedestrian. Not paying attention to what he is doing, the driver runs through a stop sign, killing the pedestrian. So what has God wrought? The murderer is killed, and the manslaughterer is now held as a manslaughterer.[12]

15. A Noahite who strikes another Noahite transgresses the commandment against theft and is liable for punishment by the courts, for the damage he caused brought a physical and psychological loss to the person struck.[13] A Noahite who strikes an Israelite also violates the commandment of *kedushat Yisrael*, violating the sanctity of the Jew.[14]

16. A person is forbidden to desire the property and physical dwelling place of another as expressed by the scriptural verse, "And you shall not desire your neighbor's house nor his field, nor his manservant nor his maidservant nor his ox nor his ass nor anything that is his" (Deut. 5:18).[15]

17. Since the Children of Noah are commanded to withhold themselves from committing theft, they are similarly commanded concerning deterrents to that transgression, namely desire.[16] Coveting the belongings of another is in precisely the same category as desiring them, except it takes it a step further, involving action. Whereas desire remains something of the

93

heart, covetousness presupposes that the person does something to fulfill his desire, such as plead with the owner to sell him his house or field.[17]

18. When mankind is judged each year on Rosh Hashanah (the first day of the Hebrew month of Tishrei), God apportions each person's income and sustenance and all forms of material acquisitions for the coming year. Nothing a person will do can add to what he has been allotted, and no one can take away what has been given to him, as King Solomon wrote, "The blessing of the Lord is that which makes rich, and painful labor adds nothing to it" (Prov. 10:22). So, to desire what belongs to another, and all the more so to covet it, is an act that betrays a lack of faith in God, for it is said, "Who is happy? One who is satisfied with his portion."[18]

19. One is forbidden to enter another's property stealthily and take back one's own object, for thereby he is acting in the manner of a thief. Instead, one should confront the other and say, "This belongs to me, I am taking it."[19]

20. One is forbidden to add to one's own property by surreptitiously moving the landmarks into the neighbor's property, as it is written, "You shall not remove your neighbor's landmark" (Deut. 19:14).

21. This act of usurping one's land through moving a landmark involves the idea of unfair competition. For example, if a person has a business in an area that will only support one business of that type, and someone moves in across the street and opens the same kind of business, this is said to be removing one's neighbor's landmark.[20] Or today, the prevalent act of duplicating audio or video cassettes without permission, even for one's private use, is an act of moving your neighbor's landmark, for one who does this denies his neighbor the right to make a living.

22. It is forbidden to withhold the salary of a worker. If one hires a worker, it is incumbent on the employer to pay the

worker his wages at the conclusion of the day's work, unless a different arrangement had been agreed upon ahead of time.[21] And it is similarly forbidden to refuse to repay a loan of money when one has the means to repay, or to refuse to return a borrowed object.[22] All these are enjoined by the verse, "You shall not oppress your neighbor, nor rob him" (Lev. 19:13).

23. An employer who works in a field or in a restaurant is permitted to eat the fruits of the field or of the restaurant's food as he works if it is in connection with his work. For instance, if a person harvests grapes, he is permitted to snack on the grapes as he works. Similarly, if he is a cook, he is permitted to snack on the food he prepares. But, if he merely irrigates the land on which grapes grow, his snacking on grapes is considered theft. Similarly, if he is a dishwasher in a restaurant, his snacking on the restaurant's food is considered theft. Even in permissible cases, the employee may snack only as he works. If he loads up a basket and takes the food home to feed himself or his family, it is theft.[23]

24. If a person steals anything of worth (more than a *pruta*) and then another steals it from him, both transgress the commandment prohibiting theft.

Chapter Ten
The Limb of a Living Animal

1. There is some discussion as to whether or not the prohibition of eating the limb of a living animal was originally given to Adam, the first man. One opinion states that it was included in the original commandment forbidding the eating of the fruit of the tree of knowledge of good and evil.[1] According to this opinion, Adam, who was clearly given vegetation for food, as it is written, "And God said, Behold I have given you every herb bearing seed which is upon the face of the whole earth, and every tree upon which there is fruit of a tree bearing seed, to you these shall be for food" (Gen. 1:29), was not forbidden to eat meat, but was merely forbidden to kill animals for food. If the animal had died of itself, it was permissible as food.[2] What Noah was given, therefore, was permission to kill animals for food, but he was forbidden by God to eat the flesh of any animal while the animal was still alive.[3] According to the other opinion, Adam had received six of the Seven Universal Laws and had been forbidden to eat the flesh of an animal in any manner. Only after the Flood was the leniency of permitting animal flesh instituted.[4]

This commandment is explicit, as it is written, "Every moving thing that lives shall be for you for food; just as the green herbs, I have given you everything. But flesh with its living soul, its blood, you shall not eat" (Gen.9:3-4). This does not mean that an animal's blood is its soul and God was forbidding man to drink animal blood. The vitalizing animal soul is contained within the blood, and this is what the commandment refers to, for when an animal dies, this vitalizing soul departs. So long as this vitalizing soul remains within the animal, its flesh is forbidden to man as food.[5]

At first glance, this commandment seems peculiarly out of place as one of the Seven Universal Laws. How can eating the limb of an animal take its place side by side with such monumental principles of human morality as those prohibiting idolatry or murder? Besides a few scattered sociological perversions in Africa and China, one is hard put to imagine who would even consider eating an animal's meat while the animal lives.

And yet this is precisely why this commandment may well epitomize the spirit of the Seven Universal Laws.[6] Although mankind is enjoined to obey these commandments as they appear, nevertheless the letter of the law serves only as a minimum, a starting point, which guarantees God's favor and ensures human morality. But, if man wishes to realize his spiritual greatness, he must tap into the infinite potential of the Seven Laws, using them to refine and elevate himself. We see here that eating the limb of a living animal serves as a hint to the potential refinement that man can attain through his eating habits and by practicing kindness to God's creatures. For what man ingests as food is absorbed in his bloodstream and in every cell of his body and thereby becomes part of his essential being. The person who eats snakes and monkeys will surely be different from the one who eats nuts and berries. And the mystical teachings state that the Holy Spirit will never rest on one who kills any creature, even the lowliest insect, purposelessly.[7]

2. The early Sages differ concerning the act of consuming the blood of an animal.[8] The Sages say that the Children of Noah contend that they were never forbidden blood as food.[9]

3. The Noahite may eat the flesh of an animal that dies by itself,[10] but there is an opinion stating that only the flesh of an animal killed through slaughtering is permissible.[11]

97

4.   One guilty of transgressing this commandment is subject to punishment by the courts whether he eats the limb of a living animal or merely the flesh of a living animal or any internal organ, even the smallest amount.[12] (The actual transgression has to do only with eating; the use of the animal's hide or any other benefit is permissible.)

5.   A person is subject to punishment by the courts for eating the limb or the flesh of either a living domestic or wild animal, but not for eating the limb or flesh of a living chicken.[13] Although the courts do not punish for this, it is forbidden.

(Note: Animals, birds, and fish may be killed for food in any way that man deems to be efficient and it should be done has humanely as possible. Slaughtering of animals or birds does not have to be in a ritual manner as with Jews.   Fish are considered dead the moment they are taken out of the water, but even so, one may not eat a fish while it appears to be alive, as this is a lack of refinement, and the chief reason for the giving of the Seven Universal Laws was to refine the nature of man.)

6.   When one slaughters an animal, even if its windpipe and esophagus are severed, so long as the limbs are still moving, the limbs and the meat that are separated from them are forbidden to a Noahite because of this law.[14] However, if one eats the limb or flesh of an animal after it has been killed, but while it is still moving, he is not punished for this by the courts, for it is not actually considered the limb or flesh of a living animal.[15]

7.   Whether it is a part of an animal that has meat with sinews, cartilage and bone, such as a leg, or even if it contains no bone material at all, such as the kidneys or the heart or the tongue, it is all the same, that is, it is regarded as a limb for the purposes of this commandment.[16]

8.   A limb or piece of flesh that is hanging detached from its original position is not forbidden to be eaten (after the animal is slaughtered) if one could have returned the limb to its original position and the animal could have remained alive for a year. But if one could not have returned this limb to its original

position so as to permit the animal to live for a year, this detached limb is forbidden even after the animal is slaughtered. 9. The foregoing refers only to a limb that is actually hanging, that is, it has been dislodged from its original position and is only slightly attached. However, if a bone were broken in a place that does not cause serious damage to the animal or bird (for example, a wing tip), if flesh covers the majority of the broken limb, then the limb is not forbidden when the animal is slaughtered. If flesh is missing from the major portion of the limb, then the limb has to be removed completely after the animal is slaughtered before the rest of the creature can be eaten. 10. If an animal has an extra limb that is located in its proper area and its presence will not affect the life of the animal, this extra limb is permitted and is not considered like a hanging limb. Double limbs that will affect the life of the animal, such as the stomach, liver, and kidney must be removed, for the law of a hanging limb is applicable to them. 11. Everything that is forbidden to a Jew because of the law of the limb of a living animal is similarly forbidden to a Noahite, except that the latter has the added strictness of being guilty of this particular transgression whether the animal is spiritually clean or unclean. The Jew is guilty only if the animal is of a type that is spiritually clean. [17] 12. Animals, together with their lives, were given into the hands of mankind. The higher spiritual rank of man dictates that he not eat the limb of a living animal. Even though human flesh and animal flesh are related, the one may be incorporated within the other through eating. But the soul of an animal may never be incorporated within the soul of man. The soul of an animal must first be separated from its physical being before the animal body may be absorbed within and become part of the human body. [18] 13. Vegetarian practices, including those of many religions (even some fundamentalist Christian sects) are generally spurious, and at the very least, reflective of incomplete theology.

Lest one think that vegetarianism reflects enlightenment, it is important to remember that the ancient Egyptians were religious vegetarians, yet idolators and moral degenerates in the extreme.[19]

There are four general reasons why a man will likely be a vegetarian. If meat disgusts him, or if he feels that eating meat is unhealthy (particularly in the modern age of chemicals and growth hormones), or if he distrusts the appropriateness of current methods of slaughtering, a person has every right to be a vegetarian. But, if he claims that it is cruel to eat meat, or he is vainly attempting to hearken back to the time of Adam and Eve in the Garden of Eden, he denies the truth of God and places his own understanding of mercy above God's. Since God gave Noah and his descendants the right to eat meat, this right is Divine.

A story is told about Rabbi Sholom Ber Schneersohn, known as the Rebbe Rashab, who was strolling with his young son, Yosef Yitzchak, destined to become the sixth Lubavitcher Rebbe. As they walked, the young boy idly stretched forth his hand and tore off a leaf from a nearby plant. His father reprimanded him for the act, reminding him that everything in creation has a soul and therefore one must be careful. If man has need for an object and can take it within the bounds that God has determined, he has a right to it, for man was given dominion over the whole world. But man has no right to wantonly destroy, even to the extent of purposelessly tearing off the leaf of a plant.

Chapter Eleven
Courts of Law

PART ONE

1. The Children of Noah are commanded to establish courts of law that will carry out justice and maintain human righteousness and morality in accord with the Seven Universal Laws.[1] A court system that perverts justice by handing down rulings in conflict with the Seven Universal Laws is an instrument for driving God's blessings out of the world. Anyone who fails to establish a court system, that is, who lives in a community or city in which there are no courts, and who does nothing to correct the situation, is punishable by death. One who establishes or maintains courts of law that operate contrary to the Seven Universal Laws is similarly liable.

In the Book of Genesis (34:25), we learn that two of Jacob's sons, Simeon and Levi, slew every male in the city of Shechem. The prince of the community, Shechem, son of Hamor, had raped their sister, Dinah, and the city failed to execute justice by bringing him to a court of law. The city was therefore guilty of transgressing this seventh of the Seven Universal Laws, and every citizen was liable for punishment.

2. The commandment to establish courts of law, though it might appear to be a positive commandment calling for affirmative action, is considered a prohibition. In effect, the commandment to establish courts of law is a prohibition against failing to establish courts of law, because failure to establish

appropriate courts inhibits the performance of justice throughout the nations.[2]

3. The only punishment meted out by the Noahide courts of law in criminal cases is the death penalty.[3]

4. One accused of a transgression of the Seven Universal Laws and brought to trial in a Noahide court may be convicted only if he is found to be mentally competent.[4]

5. Every individual must accept a legal decision he has received. It is forbidden for an individual to render a judgment himself (vigilante justice) without going to a court of law.[5]

6. In civil matters, that is, cases between individual parties, later authorities question whether the Noahite is commanded to follow the same principles as Jewish law and Jewish courts, or whether he is to follow rulings established by his own Noahide courts and laws.

Although the Noahide courts are responsibile for only the Seven Universal Laws, not the 613 laws of the Torah, there is an opinion that each decision of the Noahide courts must follow its counterpart in Jewish Law. The accepted opinion, however, is that Noahide judges and courts of law are to render legal decisions according to their own laws and principles of law.

7. Arbitration and mediation or any other means of finding an amicable settlement or compromise, thereby avoiding a court trial, is desirable, and, more than that, it is a commandment to seek compromise.

8. Circumstantial evidence is admissible in the Noahide courts of law.

9. The Children of Noah are responsible for knowledge of the Seven Universal Laws, and therefore one does not have to be warned that he is committing a transgression in order to be accused in a court of law.[6]

10. It is forbidden for a court to have compassion on a murderer, saying that since one person has already been killed, what purpose could there be in killing another? And the court

102

may not delay the execution because of compassion.[7]

11. Similarly, in financial litigation, the court may not have mercy on a poor person, taking the attitude that a rich plaintiff has an obligation to support the poor, therefore finding for the poor defendant so that he will be supported with an honorable livelihood.

12. It is similarly forbidden to pay prejudicial respect to a great person. If two litigants appear in court, one a great wise man and the other a simple person, the judge may not ask about the welfare of the great one nor express pleasure at being in his presence in any way, nor give him honor in any way. Otherwise, the arguments of the simple person would be stifled. He would think, "What's the use anyway?" The judge must not favor either party until judgment is finished. And the sages warn that a judge must not think that since the litigant is so great a person, it is unseemly to embarrass him or see him in his embarrassment.

13. If two litigants appear in court, and one is a righteous person while the other is a wicked person, the judge should not presume that the wicked person will not tell the truth, nor presume that he will not change his ways, and therefore the judgment should go against him.[8]

14. One should not judge unrighteously, acquitting the guilty and condemning the innocent. And a judge who delays the judgment, lengthening the time of the testimony or cross-examination, in order to cause either of the litigants to suffer, falls under the ruling of judging unrighteously.[9]

15. One who judges haughtily, without fearing his awesome responsibility and without due deliberation, and then comes to a decision quickly before he has taken the time to carefully consider the case, is considered stupid, wicked, and coarsely egotistical.[10]

16. The courts should not establish a standard judgment by which numerous cases may be judged according to a precedent

system, but should consider each case individually on its own unique merits.[11] (Note: Precedent in legal cases may be followed as guidelines, however.)

17. A case concerning a large sum of money and a case concerning a small amount of money should be given equal and individual consideration.[12]

18. It is a positive commandment to deliver a righteous judgment, treating the two claimants equally in every respect. The judge may not permit one to explain his case at great length while telling the other to keep his words brief. Nor should the judge be pleasant and smile at one while being short and gruff to the other.[13]

19. A judge is forbidden to take a bribe. Bribery will certainly corrupt any judgment. A judge who takes a bribe is obligated to return the bribe if the giver demands it.[14]

20. It is also forbidden to offer a bribe to a judge.[15] The category of bribery is not limited to money, but includes any type of gift or favor.[16]

21. Any judge who sits in judgment and attempts to magnify his importance, even in order to increase the wages of his bailiff or the court clerk, is in the category of one who leans after the wrong things. Once a judge was entering a boat to cross a river. A man who had a case in litigation before the judge was on the boat and stretched out his hand to help the judge aboard. The judge told him, "Behold, I am disqualified to judge your case."

*   *   *   *

(Note: The goal of justice is to function as impartially and righteously as possible, to the ultimate degree. The following section delineates some of the details of the standards of the Jewish *Bet Din*, the ecclesiastical court. The Noahide courts are not obligated to follow these rules, but must be acquainted with them as points of reference.)

22. Two litigants appear before a judge. One is dressed very elegantly with expensive clothing and the other is wearing the clothes of a pauper. The judge should tell the elegantly dressed one, "You should clothe the other one until he is dressed as elegantly as you are, or you should clothe yourself to appear as he does, and then you can enter judgment with him." [17]

23. The litigants should both sit or stand; it is improper for one to stand and the other to sit. If the judge wishes to seat them both, he may do so. If they sit, they should sit side by side, neither one higher than the other, and they may so sit during the entire time that the judge is listening to the case. But when the judge's decision is being announced, then both litigants should be standing. The "decision" is the judge's announcement finding for the defendant and against the plaintiff or for the plaintiff and against the defendant. Witnesses for either side should always stand during testimony. [18]

24. If there are many cases before the judge, the case of an orphan should precede the case of a widow, and the case of a widow should precede the case of a Torah scholar, and the case of a scholar should precede the case of an unlearned man, and the case of a woman should precede the case of a man, for a woman's embarrassment is greater. [19]

25. It is forbidden for the judge to hear the plea of one of the litigants unless the other one is also present. To listen to even one word of the case itself is forbidden. And we warn the litigant that he should not allow his words to be heard before the other litigant arrives. [20]

26. The judge may not hear testimony through an interpreter or a translator, as the truth is reached only by hearing the words of the litigants themselves. He must understand the language of the litigants and hear their testimony and proofs. If the judge does not speak their language fluently, he may use an interpreter to reply to the litigants to inform them of the judgment and the reason he found for this one and against that one. [21]

27. The judge must hear the arguments of the litigants, then review the arguments in their presence to be sure that he understands them clearly. Then he righteously decides the case in his heart, and afterward he reaches the final decision.[22]

28. The judge should not defend the words of the litigant, but he should sit silently as each litigant says what he feels he must. And the judge should not instruct either of the litigants in his presentation of any argument.[23]

29. If the judge sees a favorable point in the case of either of the litigants and the litigant does not know how to bring forth the point, or gets angry and confused to the point of being unable to state his case clearly, the judge may come to his aid slightly and put him on the right track to state the beginning of his case. But the judge must be careful of how he does this so as to avoid instructing the litigant in how to present a meritorious case, for if the judge did this, he would be perverting justice.[24]

30. Prior to the judge's hearing the case, if he feels personally threatened by either of the litigants, he may refuse to sit in judgment. But if he has already heard their words and knows which way the judgment is leaning, it is not proper for the judge to refuse to pass judgment out of fear of one of the litigants.[25]

31. If there is more than one judge in a case, it is forbidden for any of them to say after the trial, "I judged in your merit, but my colleagues found against you and inasmuch as they were the majority, what could I do?"[26]

32. A judge is forbidden to sit in judgment with a colleague whom he knows to be a thief or a wicked person. He must not sit in judgment with another until he knows with whom he is sitting. And no one should sign a contract until he knows with whom he is signing.[27]

33. A judge is forbidden to judge someone he loves, even though it is less than a great abiding love. Nor can he judge one he hates, even though the person is not his enemy. Ideally,

the litigants should be equal in the eyes and heart of the judge. If he recognizes neither them nor their deeds, he can render the most honest judgment possible.[28]

34. Men of learning who are contemptuous of each other should not judge a case together. The judgment is likely to be distorted, as the contempt would incline one to contradict the opinions of the other.[29]

35. A judge should imagine himself with a sword resting on his neck and the Pit of Hell open below him. And he should know Who is the Judge and in front of Whom he judges, and Who will seek retribution from him if he strays from the truth.[30]

36. If a judge feels deeply in his heart that one of the litigants is in the right, and there is no proof for it, or if the judge feels that there is deception and trickery afoot by one of the litigants or with one of the witnesses, and there is no proof for it, or if he feels he cannot rely on the words of the witnesses even if he is not able to disqualify them, or if another similar situation arises, then this judge must disqualify himself from the case and be replaced by one who can judge with a whole heart in the matter. But if the judge knows for sure that one of the witnesses is lying, he should not remove himself from the case, but judge it according to his understanding of the truth. And all these things are matters of the heart.[31]

37. If a judge errs in his decision in a financial matter, he should retract his decision, restore everything to its original status, and retry the case. If it is not possible to retract and restore, for instance, one of the litigants went to a foreign land and took the money awarded him, or the like, then the judge is held harmless from making restitution of the money. It is clear that he had no intention of causing damage.[32]

38. Every judge should possess the following seven attributes:
Wisdom
Humility
Fear of Heaven

Fear of sin
Contempt for money
Love of truth
Beloved by his fellow man
A good reputation[33]

39. When is one beloved by his fellow man? When he views things in a favorable light and is humble, and he speaks and conducts business in a pleasant manner. He should be meticulous in fulfilling the commandments of God, and he should have conquered his evil inclination to the point that he is without blemish. His name should serve as an outstanding model for the generation. He should be courageous in order to exact a righteous judgment against strong-willed wrongdoers. Money should not be precious to him so that he will not chase after it, for it is taught that if one desires to be rich, poverty will come upon him. He should not need to be exhorted to strive after truth, but should pursue truth from his own desire for it. He must love truth and despise whatever opposes truth. And he must flee from all forms of transgression.

40. If a judge who possesses all these noble attributes cannot be found, then one should strive to find one who meets as many of these requirements as possible.

PART TWO

1. A person may be convicted in a Noahide court by the testimony of a single witness, but only if the witness is known to be righteous.[34] If the character of the witness is not known, it takes two witnesses to be able to convict the accused. It is permissible for the witnesses as well as the judge to be relatives of the accused.[35]

2. A person may testify against himself in a court of law,[36] but since he is the accused, his character is definitely in question, and a second witness is necessary to be able to convict him.

Chapter Twelve
Honoring Father & Mother

1. Although the Children of Noah are not commanded to honor father and mother, they have accepted the obligation of performing this meritorious act from the beginning of time and have distinguished themselves through the ages with this righteous behavior.[1]

The Talmud[2] tells the story of Doma ben Nessina, one of the Children of Noah who excelled in the performance of honoring his father to the highest degree. Doma ben Nessina lived in a small village, and it was learned by the Sages of Israel that he had possession of a rare gem that the Sages wanted for the Holy Temple. They traveled to Doma ben Nessina's village and offered him a fabulous sum of money for the gem. He refused their offer because the key to the chest where the gem lay safeguarded was with his father, and his father lay asleep. Rather than wake his father, he turned down the Sages' offer, and they returned to Jerusalem. As a reward for his performance of the commandment of honoring one's father, the next year a red heifer was miraculously born in Doma ben Nessina's herd. (The red heifer, a unique creation that is born only through a miracle, is essential for the performance of one of the ritual purifications in the time of the Holy Temple.) The Sages traveled to Doma ben Nessina again and offered him anything he wanted for his red heifer. Seeing that it was all a miracle from God, he took the same amount they were willing to pay him for the precious gem the year before.

111

2. One should be extremely meticulous in honoring and respecting one's mother and father, for it is compared to honoring God. Three partners share in the creation of a child: the mother and the father provide the child with a body, and God provides the child with a soul.[3]

3. What is considered respecting one's parents? One should not occupy the designated place for one's father in a council of elders, nor should one sit at the designated place of one's parents during meals, nor should one publicly contradict the words of one's parents.

4. What is considered honoring one's parents? One must provide them with food, drink, and clothing from the parents' own funds. If the parents have no funds, the child is obligated to provide for them from his private charity funds. One should escort and help them to and from the house and supply all their needs cheerfully. If a child provides even fattened hens for his parents, but does so rudely, he will receive divine punishment.

5. If one's mother or father are sleeping and the key to the child's place of business is under their heads, it is forbidden to wake them even if there would be a loss of profit. But, if the parents would benefit from the profit and be saddened by the loss if they were not awakened, it is the child's duty to awaken them and cause them to rejoice over the situation.

If, however, the parent intentionally wanted to cause the son or daughter a financial loss, for example by throwing away money, the child can stop the parent. This is only where the parent has no means of reimbursing the child if the child takes legal recourse. Some say that even if the parent has the means of reimbursement, the child should prevent the parent in order to avoid the anguish of a legal battle. If the money has already been thrown away, one may not shout at or insult the parent, but may quietly initiate legal proceedings.

6. If the child needs a favor from the community and knows that the favor will be granted because of the esteem in which

his parent is held, and if the child also knows that he can obtain the favor based on his own position of esteem, he should not say, "Do it for me because of me," but rather, "Do it for me because of my parent." This way it is an honor for the parent. If, however, the request can be made without personal mention, one does not have to mention the parent.

7.   Suppose a mother asks her child to do a task and the child complies, and then, later, the father asks, "Who told you to do this?" If the child feels that by stating, "Mother told me to do it," the father will become angry at the mother, then the child should incur the father's wrath rather than implicate the mother.

8.   Children must rise and remain standing in the presence of their mother or father.

9.   One is obligated to honor his mother and father after their deaths. For example, when the child mentions the deceased parent's name, he should add, "May his (or her) memory be blessed in the World to Come," or, "May he (or she) rest in peace."

10.   Even if the father or mother are wicked and transgress the Seven Commandments, the child must honor and revere them. Even a child born to a forbidden union is obligated to honor and revere his parents. Others hold that one does not have to honor and revere wicked parents until they repent of their deeds, but it is forbidden to cause them grief. However, it is better to follow the first opinion.

11.   If a child sees a parent transgress one of the Seven Commandments, the child should not chastise the parent in a rude way by saying, "You have violated one of the commandments." Rather, the child should put it in the form of a question, such as, "Father (or Mother), doesn't it state in the Seven Laws of Noah such-and-such?" In this manner, the correction comes in the way of the child seeking information rather than reprimanding.   The parent will understand the implication, correct himself or herself, and will not be embarrassed.

113

12. If the parents tell the child to transgress one or more of the Seven Universal Laws, the child should not listen. The parents have an obligation to honor God, and therefore the child has to honor God's wishes before the wishes of the parent.

13. Both men and women have an obligation to honor and revere their parents. However, a married woman owes her devotion to her husband and is exempt from honoring her mother and father. But if he does not object, she is obliged to honor her parents as much as possible.

14. Whoever shames his or her mother or father, even with words or gestures, is considered cursed by God, as it says, "Cursed is the one who dishonors his father or mother" (Deut. 27:16).

15. If the mother or father have a splinter deeply imbedded, the son or daughter may not remove it because a wound may result, and a child is forbidden to inflict any kind of a wound on a parent. Even if the child is a doctor, he may not operate, though his intention may be only to heal. However, this is only in the case where there are other doctors available. Where the need is pressing and only the child can help, he or she may do whatever is necessary.

16. If one's parents have become mentally ill, God forbid, the child should attempt to act with them in accord with their mental state until God will have mercy on them. If the situation becomes aggravated and the child can no longer handle it, then he or she must leave the parents in the charge of professionals.

17. A parent should not be too exacting in demanding honor from the child, but be forgiving and overlook the shortcomings of a child.

18. A parent should not strike a grown child. This refers to the child's maturity, not his chronological age, and is based on the specific nature of the child. If a parent sees that a grown child has a rebellious nature, he should reason and discuss the situation with the child. Striking the child will only aggravate

matters.

19. A child is obligated to honor a stepmother as long as the father is still living. Also the child must honor the stepfather so long as the mother is still living. It is also proper conduct to honor the stepmother or stepfather even after the death of one's own parent.

20. One must honor an older brother even if he is only a half brother.

21. A man must honor his father-in-law and mother-in-law as one would honor any other important elder, through kind words and good deeds.

22. One who truly wishes to honor his mother and father should study and observe the Seven Laws of the Children of Noah and should perform good deeds. It is the greatest honor possible for the parents when people say, "Happy are the parents who raised such a child."

But a child who does not walk in the right path brings reproach to the parents and disgraces them in the most severe way. Furthermore, parents who are concerned about the welfare of their children should be involved in the learning and practice of the Seven Laws of the Children of Noah and should perform acts of kindness so that they may please God and their fellow man and make their children proud of them. One who does not do so disgraces the children. And worse than this, children die for the sins of their parents, as it says, "Visiting the transgression of the fathers upon the children unto the third and fourth generation of them that hate Me" (Exod. 20:5). There is no cruelty greater than causing the death of one's own child through one's sins. Conversely, no one exhibits more compassion for his children than a righteous person, as it says, "And showing mercy unto the thousandth generation of them that love Me" (Exodus 20:6).

C Chapter Thirteen
Charity

1. There was a pious man who was quite charitable, helping
all those in need. Once, he set out in a boat and a storm came
and sank his boat in the sea. Rabbi Akiva witnessed the event
and went to report the tragic news, but before he could tell
anyone, he looked up and there was the man standing before
him.

"Aren't you the one who went down in the sea?" Rabbi
Akiva asked him.

"Yes, I am the same," he replied.

"And who raised you out of the sea?" Rabbi Akiva asked.

"The charity I practiced raised me out of the sea," the man
said.

"How do you know this?" Rabbi Akiva asked him.

The man told him, "When I sank to the depths, I heard the
great roar of the waves of the sea, one wave calling to another,
'Hurry, let us raise this man out of the sea for he practices
charity every day of his life.'"

Rabbi Akiva smiled and declared, "Blessed be God, the
God of Israel, Who has chosen the words of the Torah and the
words of the Sages, and established them forever and to all
eternity, for it is written, 'Cast your bread upon the waters, and
you shall find it after many days' (Eccles. 11:1), and 'Charity
rescues from death'" (Prov. 10:2).[1]

2. It is a positive commandment to give charity,[2] as it says,
"The life of your brother is with you" (Lev. 25:36). Anyone

116

who sees a poor person requesting funds and purposely ignores this person and does not give him charity has transgressed, as it says, "You should not harden your heart, nor should you close your hand from your poor brother" (Deut. 15:7).

3. It is a general principle that a person does not become poor by giving charity. Nor does an evil or destructive thing occur through one's giving charity. Also, if one has mercy on others, the One Above has mercy on him.

4. One is forbidden to tempt God, that is, to perform any action on the condition that God reveal His Presence. The single exception to this is the act of giving charity. The Torah promises that God will repay anyone who gives charity and a person is bidden to give in order to test God.

5. God is close to poverty-stricken people, as it says, "And the cry of the poor will He hear" (Job 34:28). Therefore, one has to be careful about the supplications of poor people.

6. Every person has the obligation to give charity according to his ability. Even a poor person who supports himself from charity may give charity from these funds. Though he can afford only a little, this should not prevent him from giving charity. A little charity from a poor man is considered as worthy as a great amount given by a rich person. As the Sages say, "When one offers a sacrifice, it does not matter if the offering is an ox or a bird or flour, whether it is a large offering or a small offering, the main criterion is that the giver directs his heart to his Father in Heaven."[3] But if one has only enough for his sustenance, he has no obligation to give charity. A person has a priority of providing for himself before he provides for others.

7. The community should supply every need that a poor person lacks. The people of the city are obligated to supply him whatever he is lacking to maintain the level he was accustomed to before he became poor, and they should give it to him discreetly, so that few know he is receiving it.

117

8. If a poor person is collecting from door to door publicly, one should give him a small donation according to the poor man's situation.

9. The community should provide each poor person with at least the equivalent of two meals a day and a place to sleep.

10. A person should give charity in the following manner: the first year of his going into business, he should donate at least ten percent of his capital. After that he should give ten percent of the profits earned from his capital after first deducting his expenses. This the average way to give charity. Most respectable is to give is twenty percent of the principle the first year, and in succeeding years twenty percent after annual profits. One who is not self-employed but earns his money on a salary basis should give the ten to twenty percent based on his net income after taxes.

11. One who wants to conduct himself in an honorable way should conquer his evil inclination and widen his hand. Anything that is done for the glory of God should be done gracefully. If he feeds a starving person, he should feed him with the finest foods that he can offer. When he clothes someone who is threadbare, he should clothe him in the finest apparel he can offer.

12. Gifts given to one's parents, who need to be supported through charity, are considered charity. Furthermore, they take precedence over others.

13. Charity to relatives takes precedence over charity to strangers. The poor living in one's own house take precedence over the poor living in one's city. The poor of one's city take precedence over the poor of another city, as it says in the verse, "to your brother, to your poor and to your needy" (Deut. 15:11). However, one whose responsibility is the distribution of communal funds for charity (not just his own contributions alone), should be careful that he does not give more to his needy relatives than to other people.

118

14. If anyone gives charity to a poor person, and gives it with a sour countenance and a feeling of condescension, even if he gives gold pieces, he has lost all the merit of his actions. This person has transgressed the verse, "And your heart shall not grieve when you give to him" (Deut. 15:10). One must give with a sense of joy and a cheerful countenance, and he should console the poor person on his tribulations, cheering him with words of comfort.

15. It is forbidden to reject the requests of a poor person and turn him away empty-handed even if all one can afford at the time is a morsel of food. If there is really nothing in one's hand to give, then one should say kind words to the person indicating that he sincerely wishes to give him something, but that it is not possible at this time. (And it is better not to give at all if all one has is a small coin and it is known for certain that giving a small coin will grieve or offend the poor person.)

16. It is forbidden to rebuke or to raise your voice to the poor, as their hearts are broken and humbled. Woe to one who disgraces a poor person. Rather one should be like a parent to the poor, demonstrating mercy in deed and word.

17. If one should say, "I am obligating myself to give such-and such amount to charity," or, "I am giving this specific bill of currency to charity," that person is obligated to give the money he has pledged immediately or as soon as possible. It is considered a transgression to delay if one has the ability to honor the obligation. If there are no poor people to whom to give the money, it should be set aside until a poor person is found.

18. If a person says, "I will give such an amount of money to this specific person," he can wait until the person comes to him. He does not have to seek him out.

19. Anyone is permitted to set aside money for charity to distribute according to whatever manner and to whomever he sees fit.

19. One who convinces others to give charity earns greater reward than one who actually gives.

20. If one distributes money to the poor and the poor in turn insult him, he should not be concerned, as his merit is now far greater because of the humiliation he has borne.

21. The highest level of giving charity is to assist a person financially before he becomes poor, thus preventing him from becoming poor. Such assistance should be given graciously in the form of a gift or a loan or an offering of partnership in a financial venture or a job placement so that the poor person will not be forced to seek financial assistance from others.

22. One should attempt, if at all possible, to give charity secretly. The best way of giving charity is when the giver does not know to whom the money is going and the receiver does not know from whom it came.

23. One should not boast about one's personal acts of charity; self-glorification causes the merit that has been attained to be lost. But if one donated any object for charity, he may inscribe his name on it so that it will serve as a memorial. Also, one may publicize his acts of charity if the public knowledge will inspire others to give.

24. A person should try to avoid becoming the recipient of charity. Even suffering a certain degree of hardship is preferable to becoming dependent on another person. It is, however, improper to subject others to hardship, such as one's wife and child, because of an unwillingness to take charity.

25. Anyone who does not need charity, but through deceit obtains such funds will come to be dependent on other people. Conversely, one who truly needs charity to the extent that he cannot really live without such funds, such as an old person without an income, or a sick person, or one with a large family to support and daughters whose marriages he must pay for, if he refuses to accept charity out of pride, he is considered like one who spills blood and will be held responsible for his actions.

All he will have to show for his suffering are sins. However, one who needs charity, but chooses to suffer deprivation, not because of pride, but because he does not want to become a public burden, will not die before he has risen to support other poor people.

26. It says in the Midrash Rabba,[4] "A door which opens not for the poor will open for the physician."

Chapter Fourteen
Sacrifices

1. Animal sacrifices as offerings to God are seen by modern man as a cruel and primitive practice, and yet the most lofty souls who ever lived, Adam and Noah, and Abraham, Isaac and Jacob, and Moses and Aaron, and David and Solomon and Samuel, as well as countless thousands of other exalted spiritual beings offered animal sacrifices to the God of Israel. The truth is far from the vain imaginings of modern man, for the ancients of Israel saw high into the heavenly spiritual realms in a way that we can only regard with wonder and awe.

The reason man lacks a sensitivity to and understanding of animal sacrifices dates back to a period of time just before the building of the Second Temple. It was a time when idolatry was rampant. Man was said to truly lust after idol worship. The situation was so desperate that the Sages of Israel prayed to God to remove man's deep yearning for idolatry. When the prayers were accepted, a lion of fire was seen to burst forth from the curtain of the Holy of Holies. The Sages understood God's answer. Since He had created the world in such a way that good and evil are always balanced to afford man free choice, when the desire for idolatry was removed, the balance was maintained by removing man's understanding of sacrifices. [1]

In brief, offering an animal sacrifice symbolized the subjugation and destruction of man's animal nature. The animal was slaughtered then burned on the altar, reducing it to its elements which ascended on high. By meditating on this process, a person was able to nullify his animal self, thus bringing him closer to God. And we find that the Hebrew word for sacrifice is *korban* which comes from the root *karav*, meaning close, since the *korban* brought man close to God.[2]

Since the time of the destruction of the Holy Temple, the Jews were promised that study of the laws of sacrifices and prayer would be acceptable to God in lieu of the actual sacrifices, as it is written, "We will render the prayer of our lips in place of the sacrifice of bullocks" (Hos. 14:3).

What about the Children of Noah? In the times of the Holy Temple, the righteous among them who followed the Seven Universal Laws were permitted to dwell in the Land of Israel and to enter the Temple and to offer sacrifices to God. Moreover, sacrifices were offered on behalf of the nations of the world by the Jewish priests, most notably the seventy bullocks offered during the holiday of Sukkot, the Festival of Booths.[3]

If, after the destruction of the Holy Temple, the Jew could offer his sacrifices to God in a spiritual way by prayer and study, what could the Noahite do?

The answer is a great surprise. Although the Jew is forbidden to offer sacrifices anywhere but in the Holy Temple, the Noahite, in the opinion of many authorities, is permitted to build private altars and present offerings to the God of Israel upon them even today![4] (This in no way implies that a Noahite is discouraged from praying to God.)

Although the laws of sacrifices are complex indeed and outside the scope of this volume, the following points are a brief digest of their general principles.

2. During the times when the Holy Temple stood in Jerusalem, a Noahite was permitted to bring a *korban olah,* a burnt offering wholly consumed by fire.[5]

3. The Noahite is permitted to bring spiritually clean wild animals, such as members of the deer family, as well as spiritually clean domestic animals. Spiritually clean animals are those that have split hooves and chew their cud. He may also

123

bring spiritually clean birds, even roosters. Chickens and spiritually clean wild animals are permissible only when the Noahite is offering them on his private altar.[6] When he brings an offering to God in the Holy Temple, it must correspond to those kinds prescribed by the Torah and Jewish Law.

4.   The offering of a Noahite must have all its limbs to be valid. Other blemishes and minor disfigurements do not render the offering invalid. This leniency is applicable only when the sacrifice is offered on one's own private altar. When the Children of Noah bring sacrifices to the Holy Temple, they are acceptable only if they meet the criteria of a Jewish offering.[7]

5.   The Children of Noah may construct altars and offer their sacrificial offerings in any location.

6.   One may only offer a *korban olah*, the burnt offering, which demonstrates a desire to cling to the God of Israel. This offering is entirely consumed by fire and is among the most holy of the sacrifices. It is slaughtered on the north side of the altar, and its blood is received in a service vessel at the north side of the altar. Its blood is then dashed against the northeast corner and the southwest corner of the altar, thereby spreading out along all four walls. These sacrifices require that the hides of the animals be given to the *kohanim* (Jewish priests). The flesh of the animal is then to be flayed and cut in pieces before it is entirely consumed by the altar's fire.[8]

7.   Since most authorities today forbid *kohanim* from accepting their portion of the sacrificial offerings, doubt exists regarding the permissibility of these sacrifices from the Children of Noah.

8.   One who knowingly offers an invalid sacrifice is liable for punishment.

9.   Some authorities contend that if a Noahite offers a sacrifice that is missing a limb, he transgresses a positive commandment, but it is not a transgression of one of the Seven Laws of the Children of Noah, which would require punishment in a court of law.[9] Others say that there is no transgression at all, but the sacrifice is merely rendered invalid.[10]

Chapter Fifteen
Prayer

(The following is a free translation from the responsa of Rabbi Moshe Feinstein, of blessed memory, concerning the matter of prayer and the Noahite.)[1]

When a Noahite prays he certainly obtains reward as we learn from the Prophet Isaiah, "My abode shall be declared a house of prayer unto all the nations of the world" (Isa. 56:7).

Even though they are not commanded to engage in prayer, it is evident that a Noahite does fulfill a commandment whenever he prays. (Note: In the preface, it was stated that commandment is a translation of the Hebrew word, *mitzvah*, which also means connection with God.)

When a Noahite is pressed by personal emergency, he is definitely expected to pray to God. Such prayer demonstrates a basic belief in God, exhibiting trust that He alone gives sustenance, that He alone heals. One who does not pray to God in time of dire need demonstrates that he does not believe in Him but in other forces.

The question arises, if a Noahite prays merely in his thoughts will he merit reward or must he pray verbally? We must conclude that he would not be rewarded for mental prayer as it is not prayer performed in the proper manner. Since prayer is a bond between the physical being and a personal God, one must use physicality to create this bond, which means verbal prayer.

The Noahite's prayer should not consist solely of supplications but should also include praises to God.

The act and experience of praying to God (and it should be obvious that it is forbidden to pray to any being other than God) has limitless levels. Whether one supplicates God for his needs and wants, or for help in times of danger or stress, or engages in deep meditational prayer in order to elevate oneself spiritually, prayer is always a mystical experience, a communion with the infinite Creator of one's own soul. Through prayer, man can strip his consciousness from all materialism and physicality, divorcing himself from his animal nature, and become a totally spiritual being. Through prayer, one can attain a level close to that of prophecy.[2]

And King David wrote, "Praise the Lord, all nations, extol Him all the peoples" (Ps. 117:1). This verse from Psalms refers specifically to the prayers of the Children of Noah.

126

"And the dove came to him at the time of evening and, behold, an olive leaf plucked in her mouth, so Noah knew that the waters had abated from upon the face of the earth. And he waited yet another seven days, and he sent forth the dove and she did not continue to return to him again" (Gen. 8:10-12).

This dove with the olive branch in her beak is the universal symbol of peace. The Talmud teaches that the dove said, "Rather my food be bitter as the olive branch in the hand of the Holy One, blessed be He, than sweet as honey in the hand of flesh and blood" (Eruvin 18).

"Behold I will send you Elijah the Prophet before the coming of the great and awesome day of the Lord. And he will turn the heart of the fathers to the children and the heart of the children to the fathers" (Mal. 3:23,24).

Notes

Introduction

1. *Mishneh Torah,* Laws of Idolatry, chapter 1, laws 2, 3
2. *Ibid.,* Laws of Kings, chapter 8, law 10
3. *Ibid.,* chapter 8, law 11
4. *Ibid.,* chapter 9, law 1
5. *Likutei Torah,* Rav Shneur Zalman of Liadi, *Bekhukotey,* page 45, column 3
6. *Babylonian Talmud, Shabbat* 88a. Note: The Oral Torah, that is, the explanation of the Holy Scriptures (primarily the Talmud and the later Code of Jewish Law), according to rabbinic tradition was revealed to Moses by God at Mount Sinai, then transmitted from rabbi to student throughout the ages. This traditional rabbinic interpretation of the Holy Scriptures, known as the Mesorah, has the same inviolability as the Holy Scriptures themselves, for the Written Torah and the Oral Torah are two halves of one thing.
7. The rabbis referred to are those who themselves accept the absolute authority of the Oral Torah.
8. *Chapters of the Fathers,* 1:15

Chapter One   Historical Overview

1. *Babylonian Talmud, Sanhedrin* 38a
2. *Ibid.,* 58b
3. Commentary of Rashi on Lev. 1:1, "Saying..."
4. Rashi is the acronym for Rabbi Solomon son of Isaac, author of the greatest Scriptural commentary. Rashi lived in France and

128

was born in the year 1040 C.E. (4800). Although he explains the simple meaning of the Torah to five year old children, the depth and incisiveness of his commentary challenges even the most advanced scholars.

5. *Chapters of the Fathers,* 5:6
6. *Midrash Rabbah,* Song of Songs, 5:1; *Bati l'Gani, Maamar* of the sixth Lubavitcher Rebbe, Rabbi Yosef Yitzchak Schneerson, of blessed memory
7. *Babylonian Talmud, Brachot* 40a
8. *Ta'amei HaMinhagim,* section 393
9. Commentary of Rashi on Gen. 25:22, "And they fought"; Rashi on Gen. 28:11, "And he lay in that place"
10. *Ibid.,* Gen. 11:1, "Another explanation..."
11. *Jerusalem Talmud, Megillah,* chapter 1, law 9; commentary of Rashi on Gen. 11:1
12. *Zohar,* page 73; *Yalkut Me'am Loez* (Torah Anthology), Genesis, volume 1, page 356
13. The commentary of Rashi on Gen. 18:21, mentions that the citizenry of Sodom meted out a strange and cruel death to a girl because she had given food to a poor man.
14. The commentary of Rashi on Exod. 7:22, states that when the first of the Ten Plagues, that of turning the River Nile into blood, was accomplished, Pharaoh said to Moses and Aaron, "Do you bring witchcraft to Egypt, which is full of witchcraft?"
15. Commentary of Rashi on Gen. 26:5
16. Commentary of Rashi on Gen. 37:2, "And Joseph brought a bad report to their father..."
17. Commentary of Rashi on Gen. 46:28, "In front of him..."
18. Commentary of Rashi on Exod. 5:4, "Go to your burdens..."
19. Commentary of Rashi on Exod. 2:1, "And he took of the daughter of Levi..."
20. *Likutei Sichot,* Rabbi Menachem M. Schneerson, volume 13, page 30
21. Commentary of Rashi on Exod. 7:15, "He goes to the water..."
22. *Beit Elokim,* Moshe of Trani, *Shaar HaYesodot,* chapter 47
23. But remaining approximately forty inches above the ground itself
24. Commentary of Rashi on Exod. 20:15, "And all the people saw..."

25. *The Book of Our Heritage,* volume 3, page 86
26. *Mishneh Torah,* Laws of Kings, chapter 8, law 11
27. *Torah Or,* Shneur Zalman of Liadi, page 68a
28. *The Unknown Sanctuary: A Pilgrimage from Rome to Israel,* pages 147-149
29. *Seder Hadorot,* volume 1, page 83
30. *Babylonian Talmud, Sukkah* 52b
31. *Babylonian Talmud, Pesachim* 87b

Chapter Two   Knowing God

1. *Mishneh Torah,* Laws of the Foundation of Torah, chapter 1, law 1
2. *Ibid.,* chapter 1, law 3
3. *Ibid.,* chapter 1, law 4
4. *Ibid.,* chapter 1, law 5
5. *Ibid.,* chapter 1, law 6
6. *Ibid.,* chapter 1, law 7
7. *Ibid.,* chapter 1, law 7
8. *Ibid.,* chapter 1, law 8
9. *Ibid.,* chapter 1, law 9
10. *Ibid.,* chapter 1, law 10
11. *Ibid.,* chapter 1, law 11
12. *Ibid.,* chapter 1, law 12
13. *Ibid.,* chapter 2, law 2
14. *Tanya,* Gate of Unity and Faith, chapter 1, page 76b
15. *Ibid.*
16. *Ibid.,* chapter 7, pages 82b-83a
17. *Ibid.,* chapter 3, page 78a
18. *Tanya, Likutei Amarim,* chapter 21, page 26b
19. *Ibid.,* chapter 21, page 26b
20. *Ibid.,* chapter 21, page 27a
21. *Genesis Rabba,* chapter 21
22. *Tanya,* Gate of Unity and Faith, chapter 2, pages 72a and 72b
23. *Ibid.,* chapter 3, page 78a
24. *Ibid.*
25. *Ibid.,* chapter 3, page 78b
26. *Siddur,* morning service

27. *Kedushat Levi, Bereshit,* page 1

Chapter Three Returning to God

1. *Yalkut Shimoni,* Ezekial, chapter 367, section 28. The nine who entered the Garden of Eden without tasting death are Hanoch, Elijah, Messiah, Eliezer the servant of Abraham, Oved the King of Cush, Hiram the King of Tzor, Yaabetz the grandson of Rav Yehuda the Prince, Serach the daughter of Asher, and Batya the daughter of Pharaoh, who adopted Moses. There is one opinion that Rav Yehoshua ben Levi is one of the nine instead of Hiram the King of Tzor.
2. *Yalkut Me'am Loez,* Rav Yakov Culi, Genesis, volume 2, page 779
3. *Babylonian Talmud, Baba Batra,* chapter 5
4. *Sefer HaArchin Chabad,* Y. Kahn, volume 1, pages 83, 84
5. *Duties of the Heart,* Gate of Repentance, chapter 10
6. *Ibid.,* Gate of Trust in God, chapter 3
7. *Ibid.*
8. *Ibid.*
9. *Shaare Tshuvah,* The Mittler Rebbe, chapter 1
10. *Tales of the Chassidim,* Zevin, Stories of the Jewish Holidays, story 45, page 45
11. *Mishneh Torah,* Laws of Repentance, chapter 1, law 1
12. *Ibid.,* chapter 1, law 3
13. *Ibid.,* chapter 2, law 1
14. *Ibid.,* chapter 2, law 2
15. *Ibid.,* chapter 2, law 3
16. *Ibid.,* chapter 2, law 4
17. *Ibid.,* chapter 2, law 5
18. *Ibid.,* chapter 2, law 9
19. *Ibid.,* chapter 2, law 10
20. *Ibid.,* chapter 3, law 4
21. *Ibid.,* chapter 5, law 1
22. *Ibid.,* chapter 5, law 2
23. *Sicha* of the Lubavitcher Rebbe, Purim 5746 (1986)
24. *Mishneh Torah,* Laws of Repentance, chapter 5, law 4
25. *Ibid.,* chapter 6, law 1

26. *Ibid.*, chapter 6, law 2
27. *Ibid.*, chapter 6, law 3
28. *Ibid.*, chapter 7, law 2
29. *Ibid.*, chapter 7, law 3
30. *Ibid.*, chapter 7, law 4
31. *Ibid.*, chapter 7, law 8
32. *Ibid.*, chapter 7, law 6
33. *Ibid.*, chapter 8, law 1
34. *Ibid.*, chapter 8, law 5
35. *Ibid.*, chapter 8, law 6
36. *Ibid.*, chapter 8, law 8
37. *Ibid.*, The Book of Knowledge, chapter 1, law 6
38. *Ibid.*, chapter 1, law 7
39. *Iggeret HaRamban*, Nachmanides' letter to his son
40. *Bati l'Gani*, page 4
41. *Chapters of the Fathers* 1:6, *Aseh lecha rav* (attain a teacher for yourself).
42. *Mishneh Torah*, Laws of the Sabbatical and Jubilee Years, chapter 13, law 13

Chapter Four   The Seven Laws of the Children of Noah

1. *Babylonian Talmud, Sanhedrin* 56a
2. *Encyclopedia Talmudica,* The Children of Noah, volume 3, page 348
3. The Rosh (Rabbeinu Asher), responsa number 16
4. *Babylonian Talmud, Nazir* 29b, commentary of Rashi, "And Rabbi Yose..."; *Likutei Sichot* of the Lubavitcher Rebbe, volume 5, page 421
5. *Mishneh Torah*, Laws of Kings, chapter 8, law 11
6. *Mishneh Torah*, Laws of Forbidden Relationships, chapter 14, law 7
7. *Ibid.*, Laws of Kings, chapter 10, law 10
8. *Ibid.*, chapter 10, law 9 and the commentary of Radvaz on chapter 10, law 10
9. *Yud-Tess Kislev Farbrengen* with the Lubavitcher Rebbe, 5745 (1984)
10. *Tanya, Iggeret HaTshuvah*, chapter 1, page 90b

11. *Mishneh Torah,* Laws of Kings, chapter 8, law 11
12. *Babylonian Talmud, Baba Kamma* 38a
13. *Shulchan Arukh, Yoreh Deah,* Laws of Conversion, chapter 268, law 2
14. *The Seven Laws of Noah,* Lichtenstein, chapter 9, page 89
15. *Mishneh Torah,* Laws of Kings, chapter 10, law 14
16. *Babylonian Talmud, Makkot* 9a, commentary of Rashi, "Therefore..."
17. *Mishneh Torah,* Laws of Kings, chapter 10, law 1
18. Commentary of Rashi on Exod. 23:7 and 21:13; *Babylonian Talmud, Sanhedrin* 37b
19. *Nahal Eshkol,* Laws of Circumcision, chapter 39, number 6
20. *Babylonian Talmud, Sanhedrin* 56b, commentary of Rabbeinu Nissim, "And He commanded him — these are the judges"
21. *Mishneh Torah,* Laws of Kings, chapter 10, law 10
22. *Mishneh Torah,* Laws of the Foundation of Torah, chapter 9, law 1
23. *Ibid.,* Laws of Kings, chapter 10, law 6
24. *Shulchan Arukh, Yoreh Deah,* chapter 297, note 3, commentary of the *Shach*
25. *Babylonian Talmud, Sanhedrin* 56b
26. *Mishneh Torah,* Laws of Kings, chapter 10, law 7, 8
27. *Babylonion Talmud, Sanhedrin* 59b, commentary of Rashi, "And if you want to say circumcision..."
28. *Mishneh Torah,* Laws of Kings, chapter 10, law 9
29. *Me'am Loez,* Genesis, chapter 13, page 194
30. *Sefer HaArchin Chabad,* volume 2, The Nations of the World, chapter 1, section 3, page 269
31. *Babylonian Talmud, Sanhedrin* 59b
32. *Sefer Hahinnukh,* First Commandment
33. *Shulchan Arukh, Even HaEzer,* chapter 1, law 5
34. *Mishneh Torah,* Laws of Kings, chapter 10, law 6
35. *Babylonian Talmud, Sanhedrin* 46b
36. *Tanna D'bei Eliyahu,* beginning of chapter 9

Chapter Five   Idolatry

1. *Mishneh Torah,* Laws of Idolatry, chapter 2, law 4
2. *Ibid.,* chapter 2, law 1
3. *Ibid.,* chapter 1, law 1
4. *Babylonian Talmud, Sanhedrin* 56b; *Mishneh Torah,* Laws of Kings, chapter 9, law 2
5. *Shulchan Arukh, Orach Chaim,* chapter 156, law 1
6. *Nodah B'Yehudah,* volume 2, *Yoreh Deah,* number 148
7. *Mishneh Torah,* Laws of Kings, chapter 10, law 2
8. *Babylonian Talmud, Sanhedrin* 74b and 75a; *Tosefos* on 75a
9. *Mishneh Torah,* Laws of Idolatry, chapter 2, law 2
10. *Ibid.,* chapter 2, law 6
11. *Ibid.,* chapter 3, law 2
12. *Ibid.,* chapter 3, law 3
13. *Chochmat Adam,* Laws of Idolatry, chapter 84, law 6
14. *Mishneh Torah,* Laws of Idolatry, chapter 3, law 4
15. *Ibid.*
16. *Torah Or, Beshallach,* 65b, column 4
17. *Mishneh Torah,* Laws of Idolatry, chapter 3, law 4
18. *Babylonian Talmud, Makkot* 13b, commentary of Rashi, "Rabbi Akiva says that you are cut off."
19. *Mishneh Torah,* Laws of Idolatry, chapter 3, law 5
20. *Ibid.,* chapter 3, law 6
21. *Ibid.,* chapter 3, law 7
22. *Chochmat Adam,* Laws of Idolatry, chapter 87, law 8
23. *Mishneh Torah,* Laws of Idolatry, chapter 23, law 9
24. *Ibid.,* chapter 3, law 10
25. *Ibid.,* chapter 3, law 11
26. *Chochmat Adam,* Laws of Idolatry, chapter 85, law 3
27. *Ibid.,* chapter 85, law 5
28. *Ibid.,* chapter 85, law 4
29. *Ibid.,* chapter 85, law 6
30. *Ibid.,* chapter 85, law 7
31. *Ibid.,* chapter 85, law 8
32. *Ibid.,* chapter 85, law 9
33. *Babylonian Talmud, Avodah Zarah* 42b
34. *Ibid.,* 41a
35. *Shulchan Arukh, Yoreh Deah,* chapter 141, law 1, *Shach* note 4

36. *Chochmat Adam,* Laws of Idolatry, chapter 85, law 2
37. *S'dei Chemed, Peat HaSadeh, The Set Category Gimel,* section 6, note 26
38. *Mishneh Torah,* Laws of Idolatry, chapter 5, law 2
39. *Ibid.,* chapter 5, law 5
40. *Ibid.,* chapter 5, law 6
41. *Ibid.,* chapter 5, law 7
42. *Ibid.,* chapter 5, law 8
43. *Ibid.,* chapter 5, law 9
44. *Ibid.,* chapter 5, law 11
45. *Ibid.,* chapter 6, law 6
46. *Ibid.,* chapter 6, law 7
47. *Ibid.,* chapter 6, law 6
48. *Ibid.,* chapter 7, law 1
49. *Ibid.,* chapter 7, law 2
50. *Ibid.,* chapter 7, law 3
51. *Ibid.,* chapter 7, law 4
52. *Ibid.,* chapter 7, law 5
53. *Ibid.,* chapter 7, law 6
54. *Chochmat Adam,* Laws of Idolatry, chapter 85, law 1
55. *Ibid.,* chapter 85, law 2
56. *Mishneh Torah,* Laws of Idolatry, chapter 7, law 8
57. *Ibid.,* chapter 7, law 9
58. *Ibid.,* chapter 7, law 16
59. *Ibid.,* chapter 7, law 17
60. *Chochmat Adam,* Laws of Idolatry, chapter 86, law 3
61. *Ibid.,* chapter 84, law 9
62. *Ibid.,* chapter 84, law 10
63. *Mishneh Torah,* Laws of Idolatry, chapter 8, law 1
64. *Ibid.,* chapter 8, law 2
65. *Ibid.,* chapter 8, law 3
66. *Ibid.,* chapter 8, law 4
67. *Chochmat Adam,* Laws of Idolatry, chapter 84, law 15
68. *Ibid.,* chapter 84, law 16
69. *Mishneh Torah,* Laws of Idolatry, chapter 8, law 5
70. *Ibid.,* chapter 8, law 6
71. *Ibid.,* chapter 8, law 10
72. *Ibid.,* chapter 8, law 8

73. *Chochmat Adam,* Laws of Idolatry, chapter 84, law 5
74. *Mishneh Torah,* Laws of Idolatry, chapter 8, law 9
75. *Chochmat Adam,* Laws of Idolatry, chapter 84, law 12
76. *Mishneh Torah,* Laws of Idolatry, chapter 8, law 10
77. *Ibid.,* Laws of Idolatry, chapter 8, law 11
78. *Ibid.,* chapter 8, law 12
79. *Ibid.,* chapter 6, law 1
80. *Ibid.,* chapter 6, law 2
81. *Babylonian Talmud, Sanhedrin* 56b, commentary of the Meiri; *Mishneh Torah,* Laws of Idolatry, chapter 11, law 4
82. *Ibid.,* see Raavad's commentary on this law in the *Mishneh Torah*
83. *Kitzur Shulchan Arukh,* chapter 166, law 2
84. *Mishneh Torah,* Laws of Idolatry, chapter 11, law 4
85. *Ibid.,* chapter 11, law 5 (see Raavad's commentary on this law)
86. *Mishneh Torah,* Laws of Idolatry, chapter 11, law 6
87. *Ibid.,* chapter 11, law 9
88. *Ibid.,* chapter 11, law 7
89. *Ibid.,* chapter 11, law 8
90. *Ibid.,* chapter 11, law 9
91. *Ibid.,* chapter 11, law 10
92. *Ibid.,* chapter 11, law 11
93. *Ibid.,* chapter 11, law 12
94. *Ibid.,* chapter 11, law 13
95. *Ibid.;* chapter 11, law 14
96. *Ibid.,* chapter 11, law 15
97. *Ibid.,* chapter 11, law 16
98. Deut. 18:13, commentary of Rashbam (Rabbi Shmuel ben Meir)

Chapter Six   Blasphemy

1. *Sefer Hahinnukh,* Commandment 70
2. *Mishnah Sanhedrin,* 7:5
3. *Babylonian Talmud, Sanhedrin* 60a
4. *Shulchan Arukh, Yoreh Deah,* 340, law 37
5. *Book of Commandments,* Rambam (Maimonides), Negative Commandment 317
6. *Mishnah Brachot,* 9:5
7. *Ibid.,* 9:2; *Shulchan Arukh, Orach Chaim,* chapter 222, law 2

8. *Mishneh Torah,* Laws of Kings, chapter 10, law 7, *Mishneh l'Melech,* "I saw…"
9. *Jerusalem Talmud, Nazir,* chapter 9, law 1, *Pnei Moshe,* "Israel should not delay…"
10. *Mishneh Torah,* Laws of Kings, chapter 9, law 3
11. *Ibid.,* Laws of Idolatry, chapter 2, law 6
12. *Ibid.,* law 9
13. Job 11:9
14. *Horev,* Rabbi S. R. Hirsch, chapter 90, notes 582-584
15. *Ibid.,* chapter 53, notes 386-392

Chapter Seven   Murder

1. *Mishneh Torah,* Laws of Kings, chapter 9, law 4
2. *Shulchan Arukh, Yoreh Deah,* chapter 305, law 23
3. *Babylonian Talmud, Sanhedrin 57b*
4. *Mishneh Torah,* Laws of Kings, chapter 9, law 4
5. *Ibid.,* Laws of Wounds and Damages, chapter 8, law 10, see commentary of *Mishneh l'Melech*
6. *Babylonian Talmud, Sanhedrin 59a, Tosefos,* "There is nothing known…"
7. *Bereshit Rabba,* chapter 34; *Mishneh Torah,* Laws of Murder and Guarding the Soul, chapter 2, law 2
8. *Ibid.,* Laws of Kings, chapter 10, law 2
9. Gen. 9:5, commentary of Rashi
10. *Mishneh Torah,* Laws of Kings, chapter 10, law 1; Laws of Murder and Guarding the Soul, chapter 5, laws 3 and 4
11. *Shulchan Arukh, Even HaEzer,* chapter 23, law 5, the RaMoh (Rabbi Moses Isserles)
12. *Babylonian Talmud, Sanhedrin 59b, Tosefos,* "Behold, be fruitful and multiply." .
13. *Mishneh Torah,* Laws of Kings, chapter 10, law 7, *Mishneh l'Melech,* "We return to the words of the Rashbah…"

Chapter Eight   Sexual Relations

1. Gen. 2:24, commentary of Rashi
2. *Mishneh Torah,* Laws of Kings, chapter 9, law 5

3. *Babylonian Talmud, Sanhedrin* 58a
4. *Mishneh Torah,* Laws of Kings, chapter 9, law 6
5. *Babylonian Talmud, Sanhedrin* 58b, commentary of Rashi, "And some learn a mother-in-law..."
6. *Babylonian Talmud, Yebamot* 98a, commentary of Ramban (Nachmanides)
7. *Mishneh Torah,* Laws of Kings, chapter 9, law 6
8. *Babylonian Talmud, Sanhedrin* 57b
9. *Mishneh Torah,* Laws of Women, chapter 1, law 1, commentary of the *Maggid Mishneh*
10. *Mishneh Torah,* Laws of Kings, chapter 9, law 7
11. *Mishneh Torah,* Laws of Kings, chapter 9, law 7, commentary of *Kessef Mishneh*
12. *Jerusalem Talmud, Kiddushin,* chapter 1, law 1
13. *Beit Habechira* on *Sanhedrin,* page 227
14. *Mishneh Torah,* Laws of Kings, chapter 9, law 7
15. *Ibid.,* law 7
16. *Babylonian Talmud, Sanhedrin* 58b, commentary of Rabbeinu Nissim
17. *Mishneh Torah,* Laws of Kings, chapter 9, law 8
18. *Bereshit Rabba,* chapter 18, opinion of Rav Yochanan
19. *Mishneh Torah,* Laws of Forbidden Relationships, chapter 21, law 1
20. *Ibid.,* law 2
21. *Ibid.,* Laws of Kings, chapter 9, law 6
22. *Rights or Ills,* adapted from the works of the Lubavitcher Rebbe, Rabbi Menachem M. Schneerson
23. *Babylonian Talmud, Yebamot* 98a, commentary of Rashi, "Behold, the rabbis say..."
24. *Mishneh Torah,* Laws of Forbidden Relationships, chapter 14, law 10
25. *Babylonian Talmud, Sanhedrin* 58b, commentary of Ramban (Nachmanides)
26. *Ibid.,* commentary of *Beit Habechira*
27. *Jerusalem Talmud, Kiddushin,* chapter 1, law 1 and commentaries
28. *Mishneh Torah,* Laws of Kings, chapter 10, law 7, *Mishneh l'Melech,* "We are returning to our ideas..."
29. *Shulchan Arukh, Even HaEzer,* chapter 5, law 14, see commentary of the RaMoh (Rabbi Moses Isserles)

Chapter Nine Theft

1. *Babylonian Talmud, Makkot* 23b
2. *Mishneh Torah,* Laws of Kings, chapter 9, law 9
3. *Babylonian Talmud, Sanhedrin* 57a
4. *Encyclopedia Talmudica,* The Children of Noah, volume 3, page 348
5. *Mishneh Torah,* Laws of Kings, chapter 9, law 9
6. *Babylonian Talmud, Sanhedrin* 57b
7. *Minhat Hinnukh,* Commandment 35
8. *Babylonian Talmud, Baba Metzia* 70b, *Tosefos,* "What is this, usury?"
9. Gen. 34:13, commentary of Ramban (Nachmanides)
10. *Mishnah Baba Metzia,* 4:3
11. *Babylonian Talmud, Avodah Zarah* 71b, *Tosefos,* "The Sons of Noah are..."
12. Exod. 21:13, commentary of Rashi, "But God caused it to come to hand..."
13. Gen. 34:13, commentary of Ramban; *Encyclopedia Talmudica,* The Children of Noah, volume 3, page 257
14. *Mishneh Torah,* Laws of Kings, chapter 10, law 6
15. *The Seven Laws of Noah,* Lichtenstein, page 22
16. *Sefer HaHinnukh,* Commandment 424
17. *The Seven Laws of Noah,* Lichtenstein, page 24
18. *Chapters of the Fathers,* 4:1
19. *Babylonian Talmud, Baba Kamma* 27b
20. *Shulchan Arukh, Choshen Mishpat,* chapter 156, laws 1-7
21. *Mishneh Torah,* Laws of Kings, chapter 9, law 9
22. Gen. 34:13, commentary of Ramban
23. *Mishneh Torah,* Laws of Kings, chapter 9, law 9

Chapter Ten The Limb of a Living Animal

1. *Babylonian Talmud, Sanhedrin* 56b
2. *Ibid., Tosefos,* "He should eat..."
3. Gen. 9:4, Commentary of Rashi, "But flesh with life..."
4. *Mishneh Torah,* Laws of Kings, chapter 9, law 1
5. Lev. 17:14, commentary of Rashi; Gen. 9:4, commentary of S. R. Hirsch

6. *The Seven Laws of Noah,* Lichtenstein, page 56
7. *Kitvei Arizal*
8. *Babylonian Talmud, Sanhedrin* 59a
9. *Mishneh Torah,* Laws of Kings, chapter 9, law 10
10. *Encyclopedia Talmudica,* volume 3, page 355
11. *Asarah Ma'amarot, Chekur Din,* section 3, chapter 21
12. *Mishneh Torah,* Laws of Kings, chapter 9, law 10
13. *Ibid.,* chapter 9, law 11
14. *Ibid.,* law 12
15. *Ibid.,* chapter 9, law 11, commentary of Radvaz
16. *Chochmat Adam,* chapter 27, law 14
17. *Ibid.,* law 13
18. Gen. 9:4, commentary of S. R. Hirsch
19. *Yalkut Me'am Loez,* Exodus 8:22

Chapter Eleven   Courts of Law

1. *Mishneh Torah,* Laws of Kings, chapter 9, law 14
2. *Babylonian Talmud, Sanhedrin* 59a, Rashi
3. *Babylonian Talmud, Sanhedrin* 56b, Rashi
4. *Mishneh Torah,* Laws of Kings, chapter 10, law 2
5. *Encyclopedia Talmudica,* volume 3, page 355
6. *Mishneh Torah,* Laws of Kings, chapter 9, law 14
7. *Mishneh Torah,* Laws of Sanhedrin, chapter 20, law 4
8. *Ibid.,* chapter 20, law 5
9. *Ibid.,* chapter 20, law 6
10. *Ibid.,* chapter 20, law 7
11. *Ibid.,* chapter 20, law 8
12. *Ibid.,* chapter 20, law 10
13. *Ibid.,* chapter 21, law 1
14. *Ibid.,* chapter 23, law 1
15. *Ibid.,* chapter 23, law 2
16. *Ibid.,* chapter 23, law 3
17. *Ibid.,* chapter 21, law 2
18. *Ibid.,* chapter 21, law 3
19. *Ibid.,* chapter 21, law 6
20. *Ibid.,* chapter 21, law 7
21. *Ibid.,* chapter 21, law 8

22. *Ibid.,* chapter 21, law 9
23. *Ibid.,* chapter 21, law 10
24. *Ibid.,* chapter 21, law 11
25. *Ibid.,* chapter 22, law 1
26. *Ibid.,* chapter 22, law 7
27. *Ibid.,* chapter 22, law 10
28. *Ibid.,* chapter 23, law 6
29. *Ibid.,* chapter 23, law 7
30. *Ibid.,* chapter 23, law 8
31. *Ibid.,* chapter 24, law 1
32. *Ibid.,* chapter 6, law 1
33. *Ibid.,* chapter 2, law 7
34. *Mishneh Torah,* Laws of Witnesses, chapter 11, law 2
35. *Mishneh Torah,* Laws of Kings, chapter 9, law 14
36. *Sefer HaHinnukh,* Commandment 26
37. *Mishneh Torah,* Laws of Witnesses, chapter 1, law 4
38. *Ibid.,* chapter 1, law 1
39. *Ibid.,* chapter 9, law 1
40. *Ibid.,* chapter 10, laws 1 and 2
41. *Ibid.,* chapter 11, law 2
42. *Ibid.,* chapter 11, law 4
43. *Ibid.,* chapter 11, law 5
44. *Ibid.,* chapter 17, law 1

Chapter Twelve Honoring Mother and Father

1. *Nahal Eshkol,* Laws of Circumcision, chapter 39, law 11
2. *Babylonian Talmud, Kiddushin* 31a
3. *Kitzur Shulchan Arukh,* chapter 143, laws 1-22

Chapter Thirteen Charity

1. *Avot of Rabbi Nathan*
2. *Kitzur Shulchan Arukh,* chapter 34, laws 1-16
3. *Babylonian Talmud, Menahot* 110a
4. *Midrash Rabba,* Song of Songs, chapter 6, section 17

Chapter Fourteen   Sacrifices

1. *Babylonian Talmud, Yoma* 69b
2. *Jerusalem, Eye of the Universe,* Kaplan, chapter 5
3. *Babylonian Talmud, Sukkah* 55b
4. *Babylonian Talmud, Zevachim* 116b; *Mishneh Torah,* Laws of Sacrifices, chapter 19, law 16
5. *Ibid.,* chapter 3, law 3
6. *Babylonian Talmud, Zevachim* 115b
7. *Encyclopedia Talmudica,* The Sons of Noah, volume 3, page 357
8. *Mishneh Torah,* Laws of Sacrifices, chapter 6, laws 1-23
9. *Babylonian Talmud, Avodah Zarah* 5b, *Tosefos,* "From where do we know..."
10. Commentary of Ritvah on *Tosefos,* footnote 7

Chapter Fifteen   Prayer

1. *Iggrot Moshe, Orach Chaim,* volume 2, *responsum* 25, pages 196-198
2. *Jerusalem, Eye of the Universe,* Kaplan, chapter 5

NOTES

NOTES

NOTES

NOTES

NOTES

NOTES